Flower Making

Flower Making

by

PRISCILLA
LOBLEY

FABER AND FABER
3 Queen Square
London

First published in 1968
by Faber and Faber Limited
3 Queen Square London WC1
Reprinted 1969
First published in this edition 1970
Reprinted 1975
Printed in Great Britain by
Whitstable Litho Ltd., Whitstable Kent.

ISBN 0 571 09529 1 (Faber Paperbacks)

ISBN 0 571 08642 x (hard bound edition)

Contents

Illustrations

9

CHAPTER I

Introduction to Flower Making

If you like flowers and enjoy looking at them, it is the first and only requirement you need to make them. There are quite a few skills to learn, but they all come with practise and patience. One is acutely aware that nothing can substitute for the real thing, and it is foolish trying, because inevitably the essential beauty of life is that it grows and blooms and dies. However I think it adds considerably to our knowledge and appreciation of flowers if we can produce things that in some way remind us of what we like about them, and in a small way echo the same creative purpose as a Dutch still life painting or a William Morris fabric design.

The first essential to bear in mind is that they should be tasteful, otherwise they may turn out looking like the detergent variety. This does not mean that they should barely be noticed in a room. Often it is good to make flowers that positively shout, but this should be because the colours you have chosen vibrate rather than clash. The main object is to produce flowers that are effective in colour, pretty to look at, and in addition making some kind of impact on their surroundings.

The exciting thing about making flowers is that there are no restrictions. You can try experimenting in any materials you can lay your hands on. There are only a few suggestions in this book, and I am sure you will have many more good ideas of your own.

Crêpe paper is easily bought at most stationers and is by far the most easy material to work in. Tissue paper is extremely pretty and comes in a wide range of fabulous colours. Cellophane too has exciting possibilities and gives a nice finish to stems. You can also try using any fabrics you like, from voile to P.V.C.

The Victorians were extremely inventive in this way. Look out for old hand-worked pictures and glass domes. There are many good ideas to be found here. I have seen a beautiful 19th-century picture of strawberries made with embroidered felt, and a friend of mine has a charming old picture made entirely of silvery white flowers and leaves which have tiny pearl beads attached for stamens and borders. I would not dismiss the old seaside things with shells entirely. I have seen an extremely beautiful Victorian dome filled with roses worked entirely with shells, and nothing could have conveyed more perfectly a feeling for flowers.

Fig. 1. Victorian flower picture

12

So my advice is to be adventurous—even mad. Make enormous flowers that really wake people up. Do not be afraid to use unexpected colours and you may be surprised to find yourself making violet poppies, turquoise roses, green flowers and coloured leaves.

It is often very helpful to relate what you make to something real. A useful thing to do is to start a collection of 'props'. This will cost you nothing if you like walking in the country. Pick up anything that looks interesting and unusual. A clump of moss will still be decorative even when it has dried out. Fish out driftwood from canals or streams and cut down clusters of dead twisted ivy stems from trees. Bring back chunks of beautiful rock or stone from Yorkshire or Somerset, and smooth pebbles collected from the beach in the summer holidays.

The best tree bark of all is stripped from cork trees and this you will have to buy at your local florists, but do get some as it is very useful.

Although one can pick quite a wide variety of dried things in the autumn —especially along river banks and railway lines—it is worth finding a shop that specializes in a wide assortment of dried flowers, seeds and grasses from all over the world. Another suggestion is to look at the exciting things you can buy from aquariums—sea ferns (these are splendid to use), sea coral, and of course shells. There are a number of books and children's encyclo-paedias that will give you help on the subject.

I hope these few ideas will give you a lead. The search is fascinating and will give you much enjoyment. I particularly like mixing bright paper flowers with the dried seed heads and grasses that I have picked in the late summer and autumn. They both help each other. The flowers give vitality and colour, and the dried material adds texture, subtlety and interest. You can also fix things on real branches, a field of experiment often left to the gypsies. If you can find interesting pieces of wood, with plenty of offshoots and twigs, you can wire on magnolias, azalias or fruit and the like to fantastic effect. Evergreens, so often the only leaves growing in the garden around Christmas time, can easily be livened up a little—especially useful if it has been a bad year for berries. Cellophane has a beautiful iridescent quality which combines well with the patent leather look of holly and laurel, but make it into shapes that will enhance its transparency. Silver too is especially good combined with dark green leaves and bright red berries and it has a very festive look as well. If you want to make things in metallic colours you should use materials that have some sparkle. Most silver and gold crêpe paper for instance, looks very drab. Ordinary kitchen foil is much brighter—try making it into daisies.

I have said quite a lot about mixing real material with your work, because there is some prejudice against it. Do not forget however that a few dozen simple flowers arranged haphazardly on their own in a container or basket are equally good. Be prepared to make plenty though, because the stunning effect you hope to make depends greatly on the quantity (Fig. 2).

FIG. 2

Another great advantage of making your own flowers is that you can make use of a much wider range of container. You can take down from the top shelf that favourite, forgotten piece of china that got cracked years ago. You can at last make use of interesting bottles and decanters whose necks have always proved too narrow for real flower stalks. You can fill baskets, shells and anything else that would not hold water, and finding interesting containers can become as intriguing a pastime as making the flowers themselves (Fig. 3).

Although one's starting point and inspiration should be from growing plants, trees and flowers, fruits and vegetables, do not hesitate to get your ideas from any source you come across—Victoriana, Mexicana, flower decoration on old furnishings, Chinese and Japanese prints, books and pictures. Remember to vary the lengths of your flowers' stems and make the flowers more interesting by having some open, some closed, some even dying. More important still, do not forget to make buds. These more than anything else add subtlety to home-made flowers (Fig. 4).

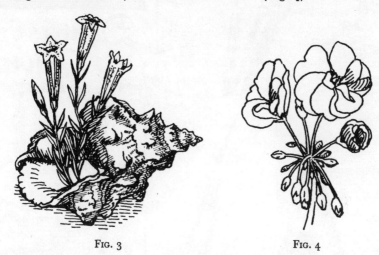

FIG. 3   FIG. 4

I am sure you will produce some good, exciting things, as well as having a lot of fun. Be warned that friends and relatives will want you making some for them when they see how gay and amusing hand-made flowers can look.

Finally, remember that even if you have spent a long time making your flowers, you cannot hope for them to last forever. The heat from the fires in the winter is bound to dull the colour and they will eventually lose their vitality and freshness. Without this they will fail to be decorative. Have a change and make some more. After all, one of the main advantages of making things is that one can always afford to keep oneself in plentiful supply.

CHAPTER II

Materials—What You Need and Where to Buy It

The first thing to have is a support for the flowers or leaves that you are making, and by far the most useful thing for this purpose is some sort of wire. It is strong and can be bent or curved to any shape. The most suitable is that used specifically by the floristry trade and is called stub wire. Most flower shops will sell you some on special request. If you belong to a flower-arranging club, this particular wire will already be available to you. It is made in various thicknesses which is called a gauge and is numbered for width. A fine gauge is No. 22, a medium gauge is No. 20, and a thick gauge is No. 18. The most useful length to buy the fine and medium wires is 10 in. and the heavy one 14 in. long. It is easily shortened by cutting with ordinary household pliers, wire snips or floristry scissors. These stub wires are rather soft and ideal for making leaves, petals and small flower stems.

If you are making larger or taller flowers you need a stronger, heavier and less pliable wire. You can buy something quite suitable for the purpose from your nearest ironmonger. It is called galvanized wire and you buy it in 1 lb. rolls, which means you have to straighten it out before you can start working with it. Once again you can buy it in different thickness or gauge. I should choose from Nos. 12–16.

To fix your flowers on to these wires you have several alternatives. Firstly, if the flower is at all heavy or made up with many petals which have wire in them (e.g. waterlily, magnolia or fruits) you need a very fine reel wire, exactly similar to fuse wire. The latter is fine to use but will prove a little expensive if you use a lot of it, in which case I should strongly advise

FIG. 5. Flower Making Equipment

17

you to buy a reel or two from your florist in a thick, medium and a fine gauge. If this proves difficult buy floral wire from your ironmongers.

You next bind your flowers and leaves on to the wire with strips of crêpe paper cut lengthways, or florist's plastic tape which is called Floratape or Guttapercha. Cellophane cut in strips also makes a nice finish to a stem, and raffia too is worth a try.

Another very useful wire to have is a very pliable wire which is covered in white or green cotton. This is called tray or covered wire and you can obtain it from Priscilla Lobley Flower Kits, Thorpe Lodge, Ealing Green, W.5. You will find this wire invaluable for glueing in between two layers of paper for leaves or certain petals which require strengthening, and it also enables you to bend them to any shape you want. At the time of writing, Dennison's can only supply covered wire in green. This is fine for leaves and stems, but not much use for flowers. If you want to wire petals you can buy millinery wire in white from Department Stores and this will answer the purpose just as well. Finally, a type of wire that can look good on its own as a stem, is picture hanging wire. If you are making simple decorative tissue paper flowers, you will find plain gold stems look very fetching.

I have now said enough about wire. The next important material is the paper or cloth with which to make the flowers and leaves themselves. By far the most useful to start with is Dennison's crêpe paper. It is strong, fascinating and adaptable to shape, and you can buy it in 28 different colours and two thicknesses. Most stationers and art shops stock it and at 1s. 9d. a fold it is not expensive. Woolworths sell a cheaper brand, but it is not quite so easy to stretch. You will find this stretching process quite an easy trick to learn. The paper only expands one way so you must always remember to cut your shapes the right way with the grain of the paper going across (see Fig. 6).

The next most useful material is tissue paper. The colours are gorgeous and are bound to inspire you from the start. Fifty to sixty different shades are manufactured but only the best paper specialists and art shops stock a range of twenty colours or more. Most stationers sell a limited variety of colours, packages for gift wrapping and these are ideal to start you off.

Apart from crêpe and tissue which are the two most obvious papers to use, there is cellophane which is available in several colours and is beautifully rich and decorative looking. Kitchen foil or gift wrapping can also provide a metallic look which can be both unusual and pretty, provided it has a sparkle. You can start by experimenting with cigarette wrappers to see if you like the effect. Woolworths gold and silver paint spray aerosols are also indispensable for instant action on stems, etc.

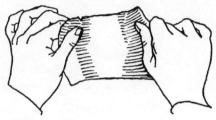

Fig. 6

Having bought wires and paper there are a few more essentials you will need. A pair of scissors which should be sharp and nicely pointed (surgical scissors from the chemist are ideal). Next you must have something to cut the wires—either pliers, wire snips or floristry scissors. Also have some glue. For this I advise one of the new P.V.A. glues (Polyvinyl Acetate emulsion). You can buy it in most stationers and hardware shops. Casco make one called 'Glue-all' and Gloy one called 'Multiglue'. This glue is extremely strong and dries out invisibly, and as there is no water in it, will not crinkle the paper or rust the wires. To cover a wire with glue, take a small piece of rag, and put about a teaspoonful of glue on it. Draw the wire through, taking off surplus with pressure from the fingers.

A few other items to have on hand are an H.B. pencil, sizal string, pins (the smallest you can buy), wool or beads for flower centres, and paints and brushes if you want to colour the crêpe paper in any way. You must use oil paint thinned with turpentine substitute for this as water colour ruins the paper. But personally I should leave any painting until you have had a bit of practice first.

A final material that can be useful is cellulose wadding from the chemist. This is a kind of mixture between paper tissue and cotton wool, and is useful for thickening stems and making solid shapes.

I hope I have not alarmed you with this long inventory of what you will need. Do not think you will have to buy all these things right away. It is quite possible that you will manage perfectly well with very few of them. I have simply tried to mention any material that could be useful to you, and there is a comprehensive list of names and stockists at the back of the book.

CHAPTER III

Study Real Flowers as a Start

Try copying some real flowers first, because however odd looking the results may be, it will be useful for several reasons.

1. It will give you a sound basic knowledge which will help you with even the most unrealistic of flowers you may make later on.

2. However well you think you know your flowers, you will be surprised how little you remember about them until you actually take one apart, and look at it closely.

3. Finally, it is far easier not to have to be too imaginative in the beginning. Often in an effort to be original you end up making nothing at all.

Choose for a start a simple flower that is not too small, such as apple blossom, anemone, single rose, tobacco, poppy, clematis or Christmas rose. Try to have two flowers, one to pull apart and one to copy.

Have your materials ready.

Wire 18-gauge.

Thick or thin crêpe paper for petals.

Thick or thin crêpe paper for calyx.

Thin crêpe paper for stem binding.

Next look at the diagram (Fig. 7) and locate the various parts of the flower.

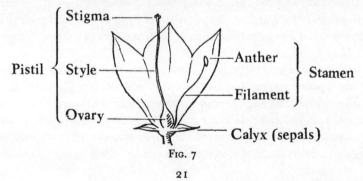

FIG. 7

First, carefully remove the calyx (sepals) if there are any, and flatten them out in one piece (Fig. 8). Put them on one side.

Next, gently remove the petals one by one and note if there are any variations in size. If they are all fairly equal (i.e. primrose or clematis) just keep one. If there are two or three different sizes (i.e. anemone or rose), keep one of each.

Fig. 8   Fig. 9

Now find a piece of thin cardboard, an old cereal pack will do very well, and an H.B. pencil with a sharp point. Place the calyx and petals flat downwards on the cardboard, and holding them firmly down with your thumb and forefinger, draw round the edges with pencil. Add a little extra to the base of both to enable you to wire or paper them on to the stem (Fig. 9). Next cut the patterns out with scissors and write on them the name of the flower they come from. You can similarly label an envelope to put them in when you have finished making the flower. This enables you to keep them without confusion, as you may want to make some more when these flowers are out of season.

Finally, look at the pistil and stamens of your flower and resolve the best way to reproduce them. Do not be too ambitious at the beginning. In many cases a small chunk of the cream coloured sizal string you wrap parcels up with will answer the purpose, but you must have it well unravelled and straightened out. I have dealt more fully with the task of making centres in Chapter V.

It is only possible to reproduce a flower with complete accuracy if you make it up in white paper, and then paint it yourself copying every detail, from subtle colour changes, to various patterns and markings. This is difficult to start with and can take quite a long time. So I suggest you begin by making your flowers in the nearest shade paper you can buy. Use the thick crêpe paper to begin with, if available—you will find it easier to handle.

Take the fold of paper and fold it into four, securing each corner with a pin to prevent it slipping. When you use the thin crêpe paper you fold it into eight layers to facilitate easy cutting out. The smallest size of pin is best for this job.

Now put your patterns down and draw lightly round them the correct number of petals you will need. If you are making six flowers and there are four petals on each, you will need six drawings for the petals and two for the calyx.

You can draw them as close as you like for economy. Now pin through the middle of each drawing, to hold the pieces of paper together, and then cut out with your scissors (Fig. 10), slightly on the inside of your pencil line, otherwise the pieces will have become a little larger than the original.

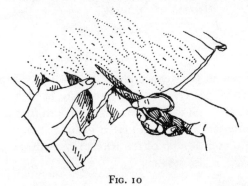

FIG. 10

1. If you are making anemones you should have approximately ten petals looking something like (Fig. 11).

2. If you are making a clematis montana flower there are four petals thus (Fig. 12):

FIG. 11

FIG. 12

3. The single rose has five petals and calyx (Fig. 13).

The next step is to select your wire. For the flowers I have suggested an 18-gauge which will be nice and strong. You now cover the wire in crêpe paper. Always use thin crêpe for this purpose. Keep it in the fold just as you have bought it and holding it very firmly in one hand, cut in strips about $\frac{1}{2}$ in. wide (Fig. 14).

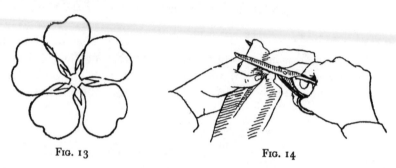

FIG. 13   FIG. 14

Leaf green is excellent for stem-binding. You wrap or bind around the wire with this strip of paper. You will probably need a fair amount of practice before you are able to achieve a tight smooth finish, but do not be disheartened because this is simply a matter of time. You may find it helps to dab a spot of glue on the top of the wire to keep the paper in place at

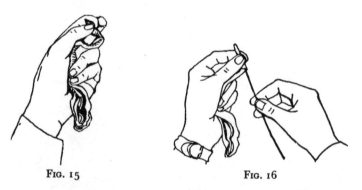

FIG. 15   FIG. 16

first. You then hold the paper in the forefinger and thumb of either your left or right hand, whichever you prefer, and tucking the remainder in the palm of your hand (Fig. 15), you pull it hard while the other hand rotates the wire between thumb and forefinger (Fig. 16). When you reach the bottom of the wire turn the paper back a little way and stick it down. Floristry wires must always be covered in this way. Having now covered the wires with paper you turn the top over a ¼ in. as (Fig. 17) close as possible. This is to prevent the petals and flower centre falling off!

You now cut a bunch of string appropriate to the stamens in the particular flower you are making. Make sure it is nice and straight, and then fix it on to your wire with reel (or fuse) wire. Put the reel wire against the string

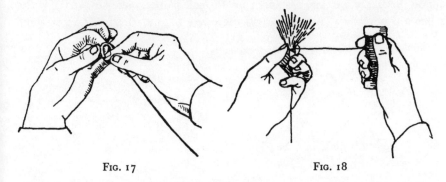

FIG. 17   FIG. 18

and floristry wire at right angles, winding it round a few times and then hooking the end over, continue winding round and round. Finish off by wrapping reel wire an inch down stem before breaking off (Fig. 18). If you are making an anemone paint the string with some black Indian ink or black paint of any sort and allow to dry.

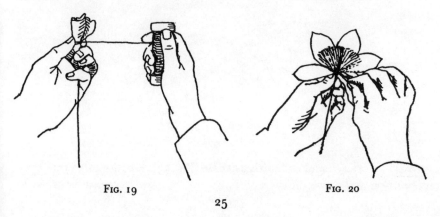

FIG. 19   FIG. 20

Next, using your reel wire, you wire on your petals in the same way. Do this one by one and keep your wire extremely tight. Position them as similarly to your real flower as possible (Fig. 19). Remember to secure the wire round the stem so that it does not start coming undone. The next step is to glue the base of the calyx and wrap it around the base of the flower, holding it in place until it is firmly stuck. Then bind over it and down your wire with a finishing layer of crêpe paper, sticking it down at the bottom.

All you have to do, finally, is to give the different parts of the flower some shape. Separate the strands of string to look like stamens and trim with scissors if necessary (Fig. 20). Frill the edges of your petals by a stroking

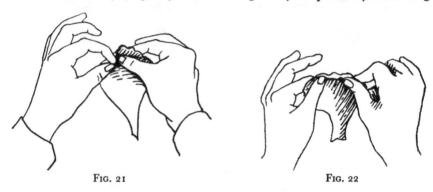

FIG. 21   FIG. 22

movement between the nails of your thumb and forefinger (Fig. 21) and then slightly cup them by placing your thumbs in front and fingers outside and stretching paper gently (Fig. 22). If you are making a rose roll the edges

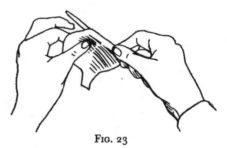

FIG. 23

over with an orange stick or knitting needle (Fig. 23). Get the calyx into correct position and curve the wire of the stem. You now have produced, with any luck, some sort of flower. It may have seemed quite a job and the result may not look too beautiful or realistic, but it will have given you some idea of a few of the techniques that are used in flower making.

Do not give up if you have found it difficult but read on to the next chapter where there are some extremely simple flowers to make which should give you some attractive immediate results.

Later on in Chapters VI and VII we will explore more fully the method started in this chapter and by hand painting and waxing flowers and foliage achieve some extremely accurate and clever copies.

CHAPTER IV

Simple Paper Flowers that are Quick to Make

These flowers are fun and very easy to do. They have a bright air of frivolity about them that conjures up the warmer climate and peasant flowers that some of them are influenced by. Choose the clearest and most bright colours and then mix them well. Put pinks with greens and turquoise; orange with purple-blues; yellow with magenta and so on.

TISSUE PAPER ROSES

Cut a strip of paper about $3\frac{1}{2}$ in. wide and 18–24 in. long. Down one side make 2-in. cuts every 2 in. With the inside of your scissors scrape the corners

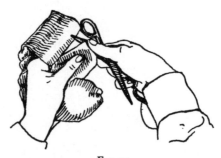

FIG. 24

of the cuts so that they curl (Fig. 24). You now have a row of petals. Screw paper at base of petals and shape round into rose. Wire on to stem and bind down with floratape or crêpe paper.

CRÊPE PAPER RHODODENDRON FLOWERS

Using thin crêpe paper cut the flower petals from pattern No. 1 (page 87). Next, cover 20-gauge stub wire with a very narrow binding of the same colour thin crêpe paper as your flowers. Mark down centre of petals with the back of a knife (four layers at a time). Put dots on with black or red biro. Glue shaded edge and form flower. Insert the wire you have just covered, so that the top is level with the tips of the petals and then wire round base firmly with medium reel wire. Bind down stem with pale green crêpe bind.

To shape flower: frill edges of petals with fingernails and from the *outside* of the flower cup the petals. Give the centre wire a slight curve and tie the flowers in bunches of seven to eleven.

TISSUE PAPER CONVOLVULUS FLOWERS

Lay four layers of tissue paper on top of each other. Choose different colours that blend well together. Mark circles of $3\frac{3}{4}$ in. in diameter. Pin and cut out. If you have medium tray wire, cut in 10-in. lengths. If not, use 20-gauge stub, or galvanized wire. Cover with crêpe paper binding in a dark colour, preferably green, brown or black. As you start binding at the top of the wire go round it several times to make a small bump to represent the stigma. Then make a small incision in the centre of your four layers of paper circles, and insert the wire through leaving about $1\frac{1}{2}$ in. out to form the pistil. Pinch the paper to gather it a little, and wire round base with medium reel wire. Bind down stem again with same crêpe paper, and corkscrew wire round pencil or paintbrush to give bindweed effect. You can join several of these flowers together to make a long stem.

SILVER FOIL DAISIES

Take some ordinary kitchen foil and stick two pieces of it together to

29

make it thicker and stronger. From this cut out two strips of petals from pattern No. 2 (page 87). Mark centre of each petal with the back of a knife. Take strip of thin crêpe paper 4 in. long and ¾ in. wide, any colour you like, and cut it like a fringe (Fig. 25). Turn over the end of an 18-gauge

Fig. 25

stub wire and paste the fringe round and round the top. Spread it out to separate the ends. Press your two strips of petals round this centre. Bind down stem. Run your fingernail down centre of petals to shape them. I must warn you that these daisies made in foil are somewhat fragile and if you want something more robust you should use a stronger paper like thick Duplex.

POPPIES

You need thin crêpe paper. Black for the centres and as many colours as you want for the poppies. Each fold will make about six flowers, but obviously the more variety in colour the better they will look and you can always keep left over paper for another time. You can make these poppies in any size you like but I suggest petals of about 6½ in. long, so divide and cut your paper into three strips. Cut the strips in two pieces and each one will be enough for one flower.

The next job is to treat the paper with water. This gives it the pleated characteristics of poppy petals and also makes the colour of the paper more natural and interesting. Fill a wash basin or bowl with cold water. Have plenty of newspapers laid out and an old 1-in. paintbrush handy. Gather and compress a strip of paper and holding it in one hand place the tip in water. Briskly brush with water the whole length of strip (see Fig. 26).

The colour will run off, but do not worry. Then quickly and gently squeeze paper together a little to allow water to penetrate and the surplus to drain off. Do not attempt to unravel it. Lay down on the newspaper. Dry out by laying on stove or radiator. (Watch out for dripping colour.) You can start to spread it out when it has begun to get dry. It is essential that the paper is absolutely dry before you use it. If it is at all damp, it will simply disintegrate.

You can get a variety of colour effects by doing two colour strips together so that each one absorbs some of the other, i.e. yellow and blue will combine to give you variations of green: yellow and red will give you orange, etc.

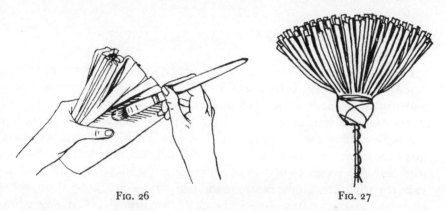

FIG. 26   FIG. 27

While you are waiting for the paper to dry completely, which may take one to two days, you can carry on making your flower centres. First, make a seed pod for the middle. Take an 18-gauge wire and wrap some cotton wool round the top. Bend it over $\frac{1}{2}$ in. to prevent it falling off, and then continue tightly winding round the cotton wool and building up the shape until it is about the size of a grape. Cut a strip of thin black crêpe binding $\frac{1}{2}$ in. wide, and wind it tightly over and over the cotton wool until it is a good round shape and completely covered. Stick down paper. Next cut a $2\frac{1}{2}$ in. strip of the same crêpe paper and cut it down one side to make a fringe. Bunch it round poppy centre to look roughly like stamens and wire firmly. (See Fig. 27.)

Take one of the strips of paper that are now dried out, and cut into four petals—two large, two small. Wire petals to poppy centre. Firstly the small

31

ones opposite each other, then the two large ones in the spaces, allowing them to overlap. You will find it necessary to slightly screw the paper at the base of the petals.

As these flowers are large you may want to add one or two lengths of galvanized wire to the stems in order to make them tall and strong. Then bind down with green crêpe bind.

To shape: round off corners with scissors. Run edges of petals between fingernails to frill them. Cup petals by placing thumbs in front and fingers outside and stretching paper gently, trim paper stamens if necessary. If you like you can paint black markings in centre of petals with Indian ink.

TISSUE PAPER WILD FLOWERS

Choose two different colours of tissue paper. Here are a few suggestions. Turquoise and violet, bright pink and yellow, orange and brown, cream and emerald. One is for the petals, the other is for the flower centre and leaves. Cut two pieces from pattern No. 3 (p. 87) for the petals. Make the centre by cutting a strip of paper 6 in. × 2 in. Fold lengthways and then fold once more. Bend over the top of a 20-gauge wire or some medium tray wire and glue round your strip of paper so that it makes a pretty rosette. Poke the wire through the centre of the two petal pieces, bring them up to the flower centre, arrange them and stick at base with glue. Cut some strips of fringe 1½ in. wide to 2½ in. wide. Cut them into 1-in. lengths. These are your leaves. Bind down your stems in natural coloured floratape or gutta-percha, adding leaves as you like.

i. Tissue paper wild flowers   (*Chapter IV*)

ii. Tissue paper Convolvulus mounted on trailing stems
(*Chapter IV*)

III. Rhododendron flowers wired on to real foliage   (*Chapter IV*)

IV. Brilliant coloured Poppies   (*Chapter IV*)

CHAPTER V

Flower Centres

It is often quite difficult determining how to make the centres of flowers. They tend to be the focal point and therefore need to be either realistic, interesting or amusing in some way. If you can possibly buy some of the manufactured variety of stamens I should certainly do so. It is practically impossible to make anything quite so good. If you write to Priscilla Lobley Flower Kits, Thorpe Lodge, Ealing Green, W.5, they will post you small bundles in any quantity you like. Otherwise a reasonable substitute is string.

For this you need rough sizal, the kind that you wrap parcels up with. Unravel it and straighten it out as much as you can to eliminate the kinks. When you wire it on to the main wire be careful to secure it really tightly. There is nothing more irritating than to have completed a flower and then have all the string fall out. To make it look more like stamens you need to separate all the ends as thoroughly as possible by spreading out the base with your fingers. A good finishing touch is to dab the top with spots of glue and then paint them yellow.

You can make your own large stamens (as in lilies) quite easily. You will need fine wires, 22-gauge if possible. You must now cover them as smoothly as you can with very narrow crêpe binding ($\frac{1}{4}$ in. wide). You can slightly thicken the filament by running the paper back halfway and down again. Then bend your wire (see Fig. 28) and fill in curved part of wire with glue, allow to dry, and paint with appropriate colour. Alternatively, instead of bending wire you can stick two pieces of paper, jewellery, beads or sequins on top of wire (see Fig. 29).

Other more simple and decorative ways of making stamens are with cut up strands of wool or fringed crêpe or tissue paper.

Making the pistil is usually just a matter of clever binding. If you want to make a pronounced stigma you need to double your bind, stick it on to the wire, and then go round and round, tightly and neatly until it is the required size. Then bind on down stem as usual (see Fig. 30).

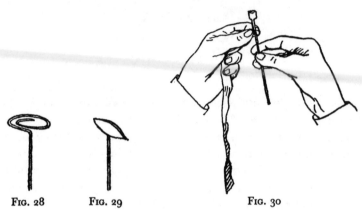

FIG. 28   FIG. 29   FIG. 30

If you want to make a round seed pod you can do this by making the shape in cotton wool or cellulose wadding and cover with crêpe binding. In order to use cellulose wadding you must make it into strips like crêpe binding. It is advisable to tear it off with your fingers rather than cut it with scissors, so that instead of a hard line, you get a good smooth finish when binding with it.

1. Break about 1½ ft. off your roll (see Fig. 31).

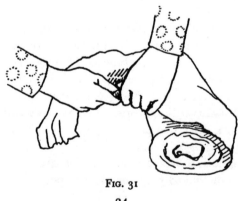

FIG. 31

2. Roll up again loosely.

3. Break into strips (see Fig. 32).

Some flowers (like daisies) have a simple flat middle and you can make this with a narrow strip of cellulose wadding (see Fig. 33). Don't forget to turn your wire over for this one.

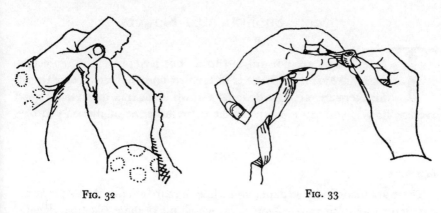

FIG. 32   FIG. 33

Wind your bind (doubled over) round and round firmly. When it is the right size stick down with glue. You can then simply paint it or glue down seeds (coriander or mustard) and it will look like a scabious or dogwood centre.

35

CHAPTER VI

More Sophisticated Flowers

These flowers are not difficult to do but have a slightly more professional look than the ones in the previous chapters. The patterns for them are on pages 87 to 90 and while the sizes given make good average flowers you can of course make them larger or smaller as you like.

ROSES

Method 1

These are made in tissue paper and while they are not particularly realistic they have a crisp neatness about them which make them excellent decoration. You can vary the colours within each flower, but you want to keep them in the same part of the spectrum. Yellow to orange. Red through pink to mauve. Green through to blue. There is more about colour in the following chapter and also a chart of the spectrum. Having selected about six different pieces of tissue, you place them one on top of each other and then fold over once. Make drawings in biro from pattern No. 4, p. 87. You will need about forty-eight petals for each flower, so four drawings will give you one flower. It is not essential to pin the paper as tissue paper does not slip very much as long as you hold it firmly together. Having cut your petals out take an 18-gauge wire and cover the top in floratape or guttapercha (green preferably). Turn over top. You now wire on your petals, four at a time. The first four you twist round into a cone and drop the wire in the middle. Then, keeping them level at the top, simply carry on wiring round the remaining forty-four, four at a time. Bind down stem.

Method 2

This method is a little trickier than the previous one but is very rewarding.

The roses turn out like the small old-fashioned variety, and if you make them in white paper and tint them slightly with oil colour (see following chapter) they look very pretty indeed.

Using thin white Dennison's crêpe paper, fold into eight layers and cut out petals from pattern No. 5, p. 88. You will probably use about forty petals for each flower so make five drawings per rose. Take the pins out and divide each pile of eight petals in half. You now shape the petals four at a time. Stretch them across once or twice to cup them as smoothly as possible, and then curl the edges over by rolling between forefingers and thumbs (see Fig. 34). In the centre of each rose are four groups of petals twisted into

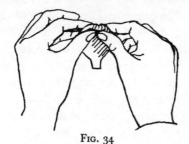

Fig. 34

clusters. To make these spread four of your petals in a straight row and then wrap them tightly round into a cone shape and press firmly together at base to keep them secure. Do this four times. Take an 18-gauge floristry wire, cover with white crêpe paper binding, turn end of wire over $\frac{1}{4}$ in. and wire on four or five stamens. Then wire round the four clumps of petals to form a circle and put on your remaining twenty-four petals one at a time, but very close together. You will need to cup each petal a little more before you wire it on, and you will find your flower has a better shape if the petals are handled very carefully to prevent the paper getting creased. You should also give the outside petals an extra curl and stretch across the rolled edge to give a more opened out effect. Cut out calyx in thick paper and stick round base of flower. Bind down stem in thin crêpe paper.

MORNING GLORY (CONVOLVULUS)

Use thick double crêpe paper for these flowers. You can make them in white paper and colour them yourself, or you can use pink or blue paper for the top pieces, and white for the base and save yourself the trouble. Either way they are very pretty flowers and have the advantage of substituting for something that is practically impossible to pick and keep in bloom.

Cut out from pattern No. 6, p. 88. For each flower you will need five pieces from outside petal pattern, one piece from inside petal pattern, and two sepals.

Now it is just a matter of sticking the shaded areas together. Stick each petal in one at a time and then finally close up the outside edges. You may find this a little difficult at first but after some practice you will soon make a good neat job. The flower is now almost finished. Cover an 18-gauge floristry wire with thin white crêpe paper making a bump at the top for the stigma. Insert into centre of your flower leaving the pistil to stick out about an inch.

Wire round base with reel wire. Stick on two pieces of calyx opposite each other, and bind down stem. Shape flower by frilling the edges slightly with your fingernails, and stretching paper a little across the top of flower. Colour the stigma yellow and the base of the flower very pale green. Paint the calyx and stem darker green, and wind stem round pencil or paintbrush to give bindweed effect. If you want to paint the flower a bright blue or pink get some hints from Chapter VII, p. 44.

WATERLILY

First, make your centre. Using thin bright deep yellow crêpe paper cut out a strip about 12 in. long and 1½ in. wide. Make a ¾ in. fine fringe; and roll the edges between your fingers to stop them looking too square at the tips. Take a short piece of thick galvanized wire about 6 in. long, and cover top with yellow paper. Round the top wrap your strip of fringe and secure tightly with reel wire. A spot of glue at the start will prevent it falling off. Cut a second strip of paper 12 in. long and 2 in. wide and make 1 in. fine fringe as before. Wrap it round the section you have just made and secure with reel wire. Cut out petals in thick double crêpe paper, coloured white, pink or yellow, from pattern No. 7. Cut out:

Five small petals
Seven medium petals

Nine large petals

Ten large petals for the calyx

Cover five fine 7-in. floristry wires with $\frac{1}{4}$ in. white crêpe paper binding. Divide your ten large petals into pairs. Take one of your wires and cover top half with glue. Stick in between two layers of paper as Fig. 35. Do this four more times to give you five calyx pieces.

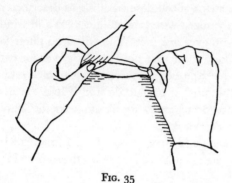

FIG. 35

Next shape your petals, two at a time, by stretching across from top to bottom. Keep edges up all the way around so they look like long thin saucers. Do this also to your five pieces of calyx. Then bind your petals round in circles, one at a time, and just overlapping. Start with the smallest and finish with the calyx. (Do not forget to curve the wires of your calyx pieces before you wire them round.)

Bind down stem with green floratape or crêpe paper.

For a final touch, paint the *outside* of your calyx pale green with crimson lake tips. Make sure colour does not run through to the inside.

These flowers are ideal to coat with wax (see Chapter VIII) and this will enable you to safely float them in water if you have ideas in that direction.

SUNFLOWER

Here is your chance to make a giant of a flower. The popularity lately for these gorgeous yet child-like flowers has at last blown away all preconceived ideas that artificial flowers were just for the Victorians. Don't try to disguise the fact that you have made them yourself, because they are strictly for fun and that is part of their charm.

First find a piece of calico or similar material with a prominent weave that does not fray too easily and cut a circle of 5-in. diameter. Also you will need some cellulose wadding, some bright yellow thin crêpe paper and thick green crêpe paper.

Break off 2½-in. strips of cellulose wadding as described on page 34. Take a thick piece of galvanized wire (about gauge 12) and wind a little wadding round and turn wire over one inch. You will need pliers for this job. Carry on winding wadding round wire but double it over for extra strength. The object is to make a shape exactly similar to a funnel with a 5-in. diameter flat top. This is the hardest part to do and if it is the first time you have handled cellulose wadding you may like to refer to Chapter IX and make some more simple shapes first.

The method is shown in Figs. 36–39. In the first drawing the binding is doubled over, and then as it is brought down the stem in Fig. 37 it is flattened

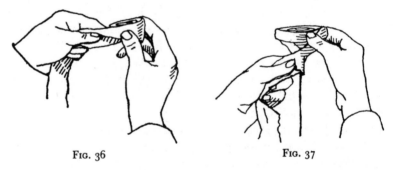

FIG. 36   FIG. 37

out again to make the base or seed-pod of flower really firm. Fig. 38 shows the wadding being bound over the top to keep the whole thing stable and the final drawing shows the binding, still flat, going round the outside perimeter to give the final correct sized diameter to the top.

Brush a fabric glue like Copydex lightly all over surface. Lay the circle of calico on top and leave to dry.

Paint material with thin brown oil colour (see Chapter VII on painting) or Dylon. Try to keep the texture of the weave and vary the depth of colour, painting it very dark in the centre and outside.

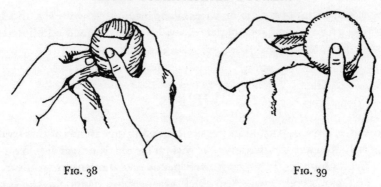

FIG. 38   FIG. 39

While this is drying, make your petals. Cut three strips of paper:

18 in. long × 2 in. wide. Small petals
18 in. long × 3 in. wide. Medium petals
18 in. long × 3½ in. wide. Large petals

In each one cut twenty petals as in pattern 8. Note that space only allows three petals to be shown. With 18-in. length you will easily be able to cut twenty. Shape them by slightly stretching centre of each petal. Now stick round centre in circles, one on top of each other, starting with the smallest. Try to get the medium and large petals into the gaps.

FIG. 40

Cut out twelve rows of calyx pieces in thick green crêpe paper. Shape like the petals and stick on back of flower in circles starting at the top (see Fig. 40).

41

Fix flower on to long cane or wires. Bend head of flower over and bind down with green floratape or paper. A few leaves are a good addition down stem. See Chapter VIII.

LILIES

Most lilies are constructed in the same way so you can adapt this method quite easily to make any variety you wish. This one is a tiger lily. You will need thick orange crêpe paper for the petals and stamens, or you can use white and paint your own. Also thick green crêpe paper for the leaves. From pattern No. 9, p. 89, cut out:

Three large petals
Three small petals
Twelve pieces for stamens
Two small leaves
One large leaf

Paint spots on petals with black ink and if necessary colour orange.

Have one thick floristry wire ready and five 3-in. lengths of medium reel wire which have been straightened. Cover reel wire with the narrowest paper bind that you can cut. Stick two stamen pieces opposite each other at top and press well together.

Cover top 3 in. of your wire three times with $\frac{1}{4}$-in. narrow bind, incorporating a slight bump at the top. Put stamens round wire so that they are all level at the top and bind round firmly at base with fine reel wire. Then put on the three large petals in a circle and bind. Finally, add the three small petals in each of the gaps. Bind over stem with paper adding the leaves at 2-in. intervals.

Paint anthers of stamens and stigma orange. Paint filaments of stamen, style of pistil and base of petals pale green. Paint stem darker green to brown. Shape petals by frilling edges with fingernails. Stretching two or three times across with fingers and thumbs, and curling over with the sharp edge of some scissors. Bend flower head over in a gentle curve.

If you like you can make several flowers like this and bind them all together to make one long stem.

PINKS OR CARNATIONS

The pattern given is for a pink but you have simply to enlarge it a little in order to make a carnation.

Cut twenty-four petals from pattern No. 10, p. 90, in thin crêpe paper (pink or white), one calyx in thick crêpe paper, and six leaves in thick crêpe paper.

Divide petals into groups of threes and twos. Cover top of 18-gauge florist's wire with paper and turn over $\frac{1}{4}$ in. Bind petals round wire very close together in groups of three, with reel wire. Stick round calyx with glue. Bind down stem with $\frac{1}{4}$-in. crêpe paper bind adding leaves in pairs every inch.

To shape flower, curve each petal by stretching with fingers and thumbs and then ruffle them. Bend flowerhead over slightly. Paint base of petals deep crimson lake. Paint calyx and stem pale green. Paint leaves silvery green.

CHAPTER VII

Painting

Please do not think because this chapter is headed painting you need to have studied art before you can tackle it. It is easier than painting a window frame and is much more creative and enjoyable to do. At first you can do the most simple of colour washes and by practice and a little trial and error, you can progress if you like to painting more complicated flowers, fruit and leaves.

As I have mentioned in previous chapters it is essential to use oil paint diluted with turpentine substitute because any other paint mixed with water will make the paper disintegrate. This has certain disadvantages for working with at home. The smell of turpentine is fairly strong and some people find it disagreeable. Try therefore to do your painting in a well ventilated room that is not much used by the rest of your family. You must also be careful to avoid spilling paint on your clothing because it will not wash off. If you do, remove immediately with a rag soaked in turpentine, or failing this Dab-it-off will almost always eliminate stubborn paint stains. It is a far better plan to start off adorned with a plastic apron or cast-off man's shirt, and then you won't be bothered by this problem at all.

Work on a table if possible and cover it well with newspapers to avoid any paint soaking through. The first thing to know about is what equipment you need to have. First, make a collection of empty glass jars—preferably small ones; paste pots, baby food jars, horseradish and the like. Old saucers that have been chipped can be useful, or if you like you can buy a cheap six division tartlet tray from Woolworths. These utensils are all for mixing your paint in. You will need as well a larger jar or tin for disposing the small quantities of paint that you will have left over. You will also need some old flower pots or tins to put your painted work to dry in.

Next you will need some brushes. Woolworths sell cheap black bristle brushes along with their housepainting things, and one or two will be handy for mixing paint and covering large areas of paper. As well as these you will need some better short-handled painting brushes which you can buy from your local art shop or a good stationers. I suggest you buy the larger brush in ox hair, which you will use for tinting petals and leaves. For painting spots, veins and patterns of any sort you will need some small sable brushes with very fine points.

Here are the best sizes to get:

Ox hair Nos. 9–12

Sable (student quality) 2–6

Buy four to five brushes in all to start with.

Oil paint is expensive to buy, so get it in small sized tubes until you know what sort of quantity you need to use. There are two qualities: artist's and student's. The latter cheaper quality will serve quite well for colouring leaves and stems, but if you want the highest degree of permanence for painting your flowers it would be best for you to get these particular colours in the artist's quality.

Here is a list of the paint colours which will be most useful to you. Buy No. 3 size tubes if it is your first attempt at painting, and No. 14 size tubes if you intend to do a considerable amount.

Ivory Black	
Raw Umber*	(*Brown*)
Crimson Lake*	(*Deep Red*)
E Cadmium Red	(*Bright Red*)
Permanent Rose	(*Bright Pink*)
Permanent Magenta	(*Deep Bright Pink*)
Windsor Violet	(*Deep Violet*)
E Cobalt Violet	(*Light Pinkish Violet*)
Ultramarine	(*Deep Blue*)
Cerulean Blue	(*Light Greenish Blue*)
Chrome Lemon	(*Light Acid Yellow*)
E Cadmium Yellow	(*Deep Orange Yellow*)
Sap Green*	

Note: The italics are my description of the colour.

Small tin White Undercoat (housepainters).

Bottle of turpentine substitute and a few clean cotton rags.

Obviously you do not need to buy them all at once. I have marked with an asterisk colours I think are essential, and in addition buy the colours you need to match the particular flowers you wish to paint. You will find the colours marked 'E' are considerably the more expensive. They are, however, very strong in colour and a little will go a long way. They also have the advantage of being absolutely permanent, which is vital if you want your clear bright colours to stay that way.

Your best guide to painting will be to copy real flowers and leaves. They have so much more subtlety and variation than you can possibly invent and the more details you can work in the more enthusiastic you will become about painting. If the flowers you want to do are not in bloom you may find photographs helpful, but make sure they are really good colour reproductions. There are extremely good picture postcards on the market now, which can prove very useful if you have not the real flower to look at. However it is not necessary to work only along these lines. Some people have no inclination to copy, and if this is true in your case, be as imaginative and daring as you like.

Having organized your equipment your can now proceed with the job of painting. It is important to keep brushes and utensils clean all the time as the smallest amount of green or brown in a pale pink wash will turn it slightly muddy looking. Rinse your brushes scrupulously in turpentine substitute as soon as you have finished using them, and from time to time wash them with soap in warm water. When you have rinsed your paint jars out wipe them with a clean rag. In this way you will ensure that your colours always keep bright and clear.

When you are painting the whole surface of flowers or leaves you will use the paint extremely thinly, well diluted with turpentine substitute. Firstly, squeeze the colour you want into a glass jar and add a little turpentine. Mix colour well with Woolworths bristle brush and then add more turpentine. Mix well and make sure every particle of paint is quite dissolved. This is important because if the odd lump gets on to the crêpe paper it will not be too easily dispersed. Once the paper is saturated with colour you add depth or variation with thicker paint. Most petals, for instance, are slightly deeper at the base and you can achieve this by painting (or dipping) the flower with very pale colour first and then squeezing some paint of the same colour on to a saucer and, just slightly thinning down with a little turpentine, work

46

into base of petals with an ox hair brush, so that the colour is blended from dark at the bottom to pale at the top. Cadmium Red and Permanent Rose both make good pinks. If you wish to add a little white paint, this is a good thing to do; but only use a very small amount. White is very opaque, and if the paint is too thick the paper will loose its transparency and will become dull and heavy looking. The same applies to pale yellow flowers. Use Chrome Lemon and a touch of white for primrose-coloured flowers and Cadmium Yellow and white for creamy colours and do not forget to paint the deeper yellow at the base of the petals. Some pink, blue or mauve flower petals are pale green or pale yellow in the centre, and if this is the case paint it first and allow to dry before colouring the rest of the petal.

To start with use your paint as simply as possible. Mixing colour is often necessary if you wish to obtain a particular colour but I should leave this until you have had a bit of experience. Fig. 41 shows a colour wheel which will remind you of what colours you can mix from your three primary colours, red, blue and yellow. These three primary colours mixed together produce the secondary colours thus:

Yellow + Red = Orange
Red + Blue = Violet
Blue + Yellow = Green

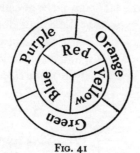

FIG. 41

The tertiary colours are obtained by mixing one secondary colour with one primary colour thus:

Yellow + Orange = Yellow Orange
Red + Orange = Red Orange
Red + Violet = Red Violet
Blue + Violet = Blue Violet

47

Blue + Green = Blue Green

Yellow + Green = Yellow Green

Colours can lose their brilliance if you mix them together too much. You can get some good effects by painting different shades of colours on the flowers themselves.

Give the stamens, centres and calyx plenty of attention to detail. It is surprising how much more beautiful they will look if they are painted with care and subtlety. Once again, it really comes back to learning from nature. The diversity of colours is amazing and there are no hard and fast rules to follow. Very often stamens are pale green at the base and bright yellow on top. Some roses, however, have deep crimson filaments and golden anthers to their stamens.

As leaves are a study in themselves and can add so much extra interest to your flowers, and even be a decoration in themselves, I have devoted a chapter specially to them. However it is as well to give a few general tips about painting them here and now, because some of the points apply to painting flowers as well.

If you wish to colour each side a different shade of green you must paint one side (usually the top) with thin paint and allow to dry very thoroughly. Then for the underside you must mix your paint extremely thick with plenty of white in it, and laying the leaf on a piece of cellulose wadding paint carefully with a large soft brush, so that the colour does not seep through to the other side. When the leaf is quite dry, you can paint on the veins. Use a sable brush with a very good point, and a thick mixture of green-yellow and white paint. Most central veins start the same size as the leaf stem and taper

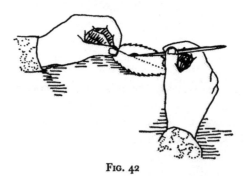

FIG. 42

48

FIG. 43

to a hair's breadth, so you must try to keep the brush very steady in your hand, and pressing fairly heavily at first, sweep brush to outer tip in a lifting movement (see Fig. 42). This process takes some skill to do really well, so I advise you to practise a little first.

FIG. 44

The numerous fine veins that cover the whole leaf are quite varied and a few of the different types are illustrated in Fig. 43. They are usually extremely fine and need the very smallest sable brush you possess. They will want a very steady hand, and lots of patience and time to do. A quick easy way out is to draw them on with a well sharpened soft white pencil. Some veins are quite pink or red in colour and you can also do these with a similar coloured crayon.

There are many flowers that have markings and they are all considerably improved by detailed painting. Fig. 44 shows a group of some of them. Use a small brush to do them and keep the paint very thick (this is where your saucers are useful) otherwise the colour will 'run' all through the paper.

Remember that when the paper has quite dried out the colour will be a lot paler, but this will come back if you are going to dip your flowers and leaves in wax. This helps to preserve them, enables you to clean them and gives a realistic finish.

If you have worked hard to make them look real it is well worth the trouble of waxing them. All you need to know is in the following chapter. Read on.

CHAPTER VIII

Waxing

The thought of wax invokes in many people's minds a rather dull Victorian approach to making flowers, but believe me, it can instil into paper a translucent quality which is nearer than any other material to the watery texture of real flowers and foliage. They do in fact acquire, as if by magic, a very natural look and substance. Some things definitely wax more satisfactorily than others but whatever you choose to do will benefit from the added strength and protection a coat of wax will give it. You can more easily mix waxed flowers and foliage with fresh material. You will also be able to clean them, and even, if you wish, wrap up in tissue paper and store away in a box for as long as you like without them deteriorating.

Certain flowers are ideal for waxing. Waterlilies immediately come to mind. Lilies, blossoms, roses, morning glory are also improved as well as most leaves, particularly the ones that have a rather patent leather appearance. Do remember that although wax has a certain amount of plasticity, it will crack if you give it too rough a handling. When you wish to pack waxed flowers into a box, you want to make sure it is plenty large enough and that there is enough tissue paper or wood wool to protect them.

Before you embark on waxing there are a few pieces of equipment you will need. Please have clothing well protected from wax splashes. Sleeves are particularly vulnerable. I also advise a plastic overall or apron.

Ideally you need a special room to work in. A basement or workroom where you can spread your things about undisturbed. However don't worry if the kitchen is the only available room you possess. You will just have to take extra care with the wax and be scrupulously tidy.

EQUIPMENT

Work table covered with newspaper.
Plenty of flower pots and cocoa tins.
Double boiler.
Wax.
Single burner (electric best), if available.

Wax is an inflammable substance and it should be handled with a certain amount of care. It should never be allowed to boil and this is why you should melt it in a double saucepan over boiling water, remembering not to let it ever boil dry. The wax needs to be fairly hot and liquid, so that it will hurt your fingertips if you inadvertently touch it. To keep a steady temperature is not easy. You will find it necessary to adjust the heat from time to time. If you find it gets too hot take the saucepan off the stove completely for a few minutes. Flowers need a thinner, hotter coating than leaves because waxing tends to slightly dull the colour, and the thicker you put it on the more obscured the colour will become.

Once you have acquired a double saucepan you must next buy the wax. To start with I suggest you buy a few dozen clear white candles. If you are only waxing small flowers and leaves, you won't need very much wax, and this will be sufficient in quantity.

If, later on, you want to do a fair amount of waxing, i.e. fruit and large leaves, etc., you may find it worth your while to buy it in bulk from a wax refiners. Paraffin wax is usually recommended because of its transparency, although it does have a tendency to crack more easily than other more pliable waxes. It is therefore a good idea to ask the manufacturer's advice before you order. Unfortunately the smallest quantity you can buy it in is 28 lb. at about 2s 4d. per lb. This might be worth while if you can share the cost with friends.

In any case, see how you get on with the candles first. Melt the wax down and extract any candle wicks with a fork. If you are doing this on the kitchen stove, because the ideal of a single burner is not likely to be available to many people, you will have to guard against splashing drops of wax over it. A good precaution is to lay some large pieces of silver cooking foil around the saucepan and this can collect any specks of wax and save you the tedious task of cleaning it off. As a general rule you wax the flowers and leaves before you mount them on to long stems. You must have shaped them carefully and completely first, because once the wax is on them, the less you touch them the better.

Make sure the stamens are spread out and in place, and the petals frilled and curved as much as possible. The more time you give to this task the less stiff and artificial the final result will be. Do not neglect the leaves and buds. They will need as much attention as the flowers.

Be quite sure that the paint has completely dried out. If there is any trace of dampness in the paper when it is waxed, there is a tendency for the wax to bubble or lift off. Having assured yourself that there is no more you can do to improve the appearance of your flowers, prepare to start the waxing process. Make sure the wax is deep enough to cover the flowers. Getting the wax exactly the right thickness is a matter of experience. You can always get it thicker by dipping flowers in a second time, but it is better to have a too thin coating than too thick. If you do find you get too much wax on, you can always dip the flower in again and melt the whole lot off.

Simply dip the flowers or leaves right into the wax so that every part is quite submerged and then lift out quickly. Shake all the surplus wax off as briskly as possible and put in a tin or flower pot to cool off for just a minute or two. If there are any prominent drips of wax you can gently coax them off with your fingernails. Hold flowers by the stem as close to the flower as possible and when you bring them out of the wax slightly swirl them as you shake the wax off. This helps to distribute it evenly. Also keep the flower moving as the wax is cooling. Blow on it to speed up the process and try to avoid wax clogging up the centre and dripping down the stem. Treat the leaves exactly the same way. If you wish you may make them a bit shiny as in the case of camellia, holly or hothouse plant leaves, simply fill a plastic bowl with cold water and as you bring the leaves out of the wax dip them immediately into the water and take them out again at once. This sets the wax very quickly. Do not, however, be tempted to do it to any flower whatsoever, because shiny flowers will look extremely unpleasant.

If you wish to avoid waxing the flower centre turn the stem wire right back on itself (see Fig. 45) and holding the wire above flower, lower gently into wax, being careful to see that only the petals become submerged and

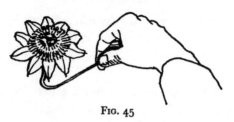

FIG. 45

lift quickly out again. Bend stem wire back again, hold flower in palm of hand (see Fig. 46) to keep petals in position until the wax is set.

You will find that waxing helps to strengthen the petals of flowers and keeps them in a fixed position. You can help to make sure they stay in the correct position by pressing them together where they overlap as the wax is cooling down. It is quite a good idea to dab a little glue on the base of the

FIG. 46

petals of flowers like single roses and orange blossom before you wax them to make absolutely sure that the petals won't hang down and be knocked off.

To maintain waxed flowers all you need to do is dust regularly and wipe over with a damp cloth every three to six months. If the wax gets cracked for some reason, just warm the flowers slightly in front of a fan heater. If they are badly damaged you can always completely re-wax them. To do

54

this you will need to unbind all the leaves and flowers. One by one dip them in hot wax until the old wax has melted off completely. Take them out, wax again if necessary, and remount up again into stems as before.

Wax flowers should not be put in very sunny windows or stood too close to fires or radiators. Given reasonable care you will find they keep their original freshness for a good many years.

CHAPTER IX

Making Leaves

Leaves can be beautiful on their own account, and are certainly worth as much consideration and attention as flowers. Their variety of colour, shape and pattern is infinite and they can often provide as much focus of colour and interest in an arrangement as a flower can. If you make a dozen or two really good assorted and unusual leaves they will give you a decoration that is not only subtle and out of the ordinary but will also be pleasing to look at in any season.

Another point in favour of making good leaves (and I have particularly in mind fairly large ones like artichoke, begonia, kale, megasia, vine and hosta) is that while you can always buy flowers throughout the year, interesting leaves to arrange with them are not always available.

You can try adding your mixed leaves to a bunch of fresh cut flowers. Do be sure to wax them, and have stems mounted with guttapercha or floratape, so that you can safely put them both together in water.

Handmade flowers lose much of their artificiality if they are accompanied with accurate leaves. Cut them out in a variety of sizes and notice the colour variations from the small to the large ones. Most leaves when they open out are a much brighter, richer green with plenty of yellow in it. As they get larger and older they tend to darken and grey slightly.

If you are copying a real specimen be sure to make accurate patterns for leaves and buds as well as the flowers. In most cases you will need large, medium and small sized leaves. You will find the edges of leaves are widely varied. Often they have serrated edges and these are cut out by a special technique. In (Fig. 47) you will see some examples of serrated edges.

You start making the leaves as you would flower petals as in Chapter III. Do not attempt to cut the serrations at first. Make your patterns without

56

them. Add ⅛ in. all round to allow for waste when you cut round for the serrations. Cut your leaves out in groups of four or eight depending on the thickness of the crêpe paper. For most large leaves I would use thick paper. LEAVE THE PINS IN. Working from the top of the leaf start making your cuts

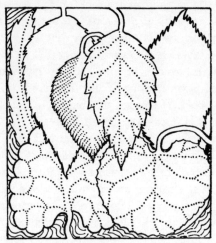

FIG. 47

down the right-hand side (reverse if you are left-handed). Use your scissors in a curving movement inwards and then bring sharply out again as in (Fig. 48). Hold layers of paper well together in your left hand as close to the edges as you can. Make your serrations down to the bottom of the leaf. Turn over and work down the other side from the top again.

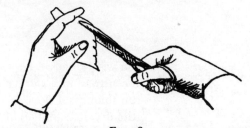

FIG. 48

In rose leaves these serrations are very small and close together. In vine leaves they are quite deep and placed far apart. It is really a matter of observing very closely the leaves you wish to make. Some have a very fine

57

hair-like edging and you can get this effect by cutting out leaves with your floristry scissors. If you are making leaves that have simple uniform cleft edges, as in holly or oak, make your patterns exactly the same as the leaves and cut out round edges with great care.

Bear in mind that a large proportion of leaves have perfectly plain edges and can be cut out as easily as petals. If you are going to wax your leaves you can make them with two layers of paper that will become fused together in the waxing. Two layers of thin crêpe paper will be ideal for most leaves. Very large or thick leaves can be made in two layers of Dennison's thick duplex paper which is very strong. You can make it up in green paper or you can paint your own. If you are making up in green paper try using a dark colour on top and a pale one for underneath.

The next job is to wire up, and for this you will need tray wire (covered wire) and florist's stub wire. For small simple leaves, like lily, tradescantia, prunus, a length of medium tray wire, 24–26 gauge, stuck with glue down centre will suffice. When cutting up wire allow 2 to 3 in. long for the stem. If you are sticking two layers per leaf un-pin your drawing and keep pile of leaves together. Then lift up top piece, place glued wire on centre of pile as far down to tip of leaf as possible, and replace top layer, keeping the two edges exactly together. Press together, and lift off wired leaf (see Fig. 49).

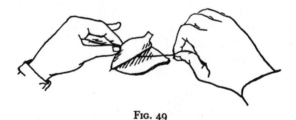

FIG. 49

Continue down pile of cut-outs. If you wish to wire a single layer of paper proceed as follows. Glue wire, lay on centre of leaf, and double paper over wire (see Fig. 50). Press down and run thumbnail along inner edge of wire to form centre vein. When glue is quite dry, open out and press leaf flat.

Certain leaves such as strawberry, ivy, vine, arum, need extra wiring at base (see Fig. 51). This gives strength and enables leaf to hold its shape. Cut medium tray wire the length required to fit leaf and bend to shape. Glue and stick in leaf at the same time as you put in your centre vein. This method is only suitable for double layered leaves.

If you are making large leaves you must use stronger wires to support them. Cover an 18-gauge floristry wire with crêpe paper binding for the centre vein. If you are making exceptionally large leaves like artichoke or

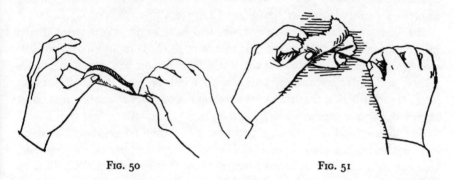

FIG. 50   FIG. 51

arum bind three wires together at intervals of between 2 and 3 in. Bind them as smoothly as possible and stick them in the middle of your leaf between the two layers of paper. When binding down the stems of leaves be sure to start off by binding round paper at the base of the leaf.

Small leaves simply need a ¼-in. crêpe paper binding down the stem. If a leaf has a thick stem bind over wire with a layer of cellulose wadding, adding another wire if you want to make a very long stem. Cover over with ½-in. crêpe paper binding. To get this as tight and smooth as possible run your binding up and down the stem at least three times.

There are so many varieties of leaves that are worthy of study that one is hard put to know where to start. In autumn the leaves of deciduous trees take on colours of incredible brilliance, ranging from golden yellows to rich crimson pinks. Other leaves turn to tawny orange browns which are equally beautiful. Many hothouse plants, which are now available in splendid number, have leaves with rich colours and exotic patterns. Below are listed some varieties for you to search out and copy when you can.

In Spring or Summer: Prunus (Cherry), Hosta, Artichoke, Arum, Geranium, large and small leafed green and variegated Ivy, Hart's tongue fern, decorative Kale.

59

In Autumn: Megasia, Vine, Oak, Brown Ivy, Beech.

Hothouse pot plants throughout the year: Begonia Rex, Tradescantia, Chlorophytum, Caladium, Croton.

Most leaves depend very much on skilful painting if you want them to look absolutely life-like. Although simple green leaves look quite satisfactory made up in coloured paper anything more complicated in colour is much improved with painting by hand (see Chapter VII).

For autumn coloured leaves you want to have some yellow paint mixed in one jar and some permanent rose (not very diluted) in another. You then blend your colours together on the leaves. Wash most of the leaf over with yellow, and then haphazardly paint on your red, keeping the brush moving in the same direction that the veins would go. You can have some neat paint squeezed on to a saucer as well, and in some areas of the leaf build up a darker area of red or yellow. Painting by this method results in a much more natural colour than if you simply paint orange straight on to the paper. You can also vary the colour a great deal by thinning down the yellow to make a pale cream or making it much deeper. The amount of red you paint on can be varied too. Paint prunus and vine this way using green and purple-crimson.

I have mentioned in Chapter VII the way to paint veins. It is necessary to learn to do this well because so many leaves are made distinctive by the pattern of their veining. Ivy leaves, vine, caladium, arum, are typical examples. A good sable brush with a good point will help you a lot. Try to keep your hand steady and complete the length of a vein in one movement.

Always start painting at the thick end and finish at the thin. When you are painting patterns on leaves always use your paint very dry, and observe very closely the leaf you are copying. Try to get the colour exactly right, and paint the markings as accurately as possible.

If you are painting a leaf that is both red and green, paint the red colour first. It is then less likely to turn brown when it comes into contact with the green.

Begonia Rex leaves are often marked with silver patterns. Paint these on with a tin of Woolworths' silver enamel paint. If you want to paint thick double crêpe paper a very dark rich green, always use plenty of paint and work in well with your brush, because this paper is less ready to absorb it than thin crêpe paper.

If you want to paint variegated leaves such as ivy, or chlorophytum, paint your cream colour (white and yellow mixed together), and allow to dry out completely. Next paint on the grey pattern which needs to be fairly thick white with black and green added to it. When this is quite dry, paint on the final green colour which once again needs to be fairly thick paint. Variegated leaves are very decorative to use in arrangements and have the advantage of being slightly unusual.

Before you wax your leaves do be sure to give them a really good natural shape. Leaves of the lily family can be dented quite well by marking with the back of your scissors. Tear off a piece of cellulose wadding and lay it down on the table. Put a leaf on it and run the back of the blade in vertical lines parallel to the centre vein (see Fig. 52).

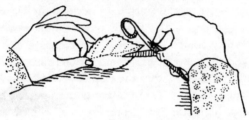

Fig. 52

Always curve the centre wire, and slightly stretch paper round edges. Finally, do not forget when you are mounting leaves on to a stem to try and achieve a natural effect of something growing. Observe how the leaves are spaced and if they grow in pairs. Put in some offshoots if possible and when you have mounted all your leaves together curve and bend the stems.

CHAPTER X

Fruit

Fruit is the natural complement of flowers. The Dutch still-life painters of the 17th century demonstrate beautifully the wonderful relationship between flowers, fruit, insects and leaves, grasses and butterflies. They put bunches of green and purple grapes with delicate moss roses and place peaches and pomegranates beside passion flowers and pinks. If you have the opportunity to see some of these pictures, either in books or museums, I am certain you will find them a rich source of inspiration.

Maybe making fruit is not within the scope of everybody. It often involves difficult waxing and painting. There is plenty of imported hand-made fruit and vegetables of a high standard from which to choose and buy. Plastic material, too, has been much improved over the past few years and the citrus fruits are particularly convincing.

However, there are simple things that one can easily make, in a field that is mostly left untried by the manufacturers. For example, it is impossible to buy fruit that looks as if it is really growing on branches with leaves, etc. If you have ever seen oranges growing, you will know how delightful and ornamental they look. They have very attractive leaves and the fruit as it first forms is a tiny round green ball.

Blackberries are relatively easy to make and look resplendent mounted on delicate stems with two or three leaf sprays as in Fig. 53. You also have the satisfaction of producing a fruit that would be most unpractical to pick and bring into the house in its real state.

Other fruit stems that are equally effective and not too difficult to make are hips, cherries, apricots and snowberry. Below are instructions on how to make them and on page 90 are diagrams of leaves and actual size fruit shapes.

For equipment you will need paints and brushes (see Chapter VII), wax (see Chaper VIII), cellulose wadding, cotton wool, shellac and methylated spirit, medium tray wire and glue.

BLACKBERRY SPRAY
Pattern 11, p. 90

Materials: cotton wool and coriander seeds, thin crêpe paper, medium tray wire and copydex.

Approximately five fruits and two leaves per spray. Cut pieces of tray wire 4 in. long, unwrap cotton wool, tease and fluff up a very thin layer. Start wrapping round top of the tray wire, turn wire over ¼ in. and continue winding round till you have a small tight ball about the size of your finger-nail. Make enough for the required number of blackberries. One at a time, brush over complete surface of cotton wool ball with copydex and then cover with coriander seeds. Press into a good round shape and leave to dry. Paint blackberries bright crimson lake and black, using very little turpentine. Add some terebine dryers if possible. Otherwise the paint may take weeks to dry! When completely dry, brush over with shellac. Rinse brush immediately in methylated spirit. Cut your leaves from pattern No. 11, p. 90, in thin white or leaf green crêpe paper. There are one large, two medium and two small to each leaf spray. Serrate edges (see Chapter IX), tray wire two layers together. Bind down stems of the large size leaves with thin crêpe

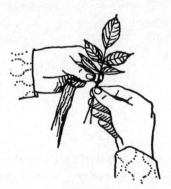

FIG. 53

paper binding. Then bind five leaves together as shown in Fig. 53. **Paint green and purple-brown. Wax.**

Mount blackberries and leaves on to 18-gauge floristry wires with **crêpe paper binding as in Fig. 54.** Paint stems with a mixture of purple and brown paint with a drop of white in it. Shape stem.

SNOWBERRY SPRAY
Pattern 12, p. 90

Materials: cotton wool, medium tray wire, wax, thin crêpe paper.
Approximately eight fruits and three pairs of leaves per spray.

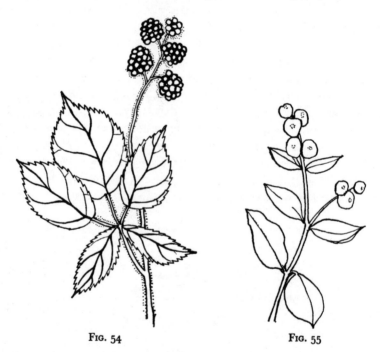

FIG. 54   FIG. 55

Unwrap cotton wool, tease, and fluff up a very thin layer. Start **wrapping round top of tray wire, turn wire over ¼ in. and continue winding round until you have a small tight ball.** These can vary a little in size, but should

v. Roses, in tissue paper on the left and crêpe paper on the right (*Chapter IV*)

vi. Morning Glory, painted blue (*Chapter VI*)

VII. Examples of waxed Christmas Roses, leaves and fruit

not become any larger than a fingernail. Your next job is to cover them in a thick coat of wax. Fortunately the berries themselves are extremely irregular in shape (see Fig. 55), so you do not have to be too skilful. It is important however to have the wax really clean and very thick. Melt it down in the usual way and then take off heat. When a thick skin has formed, put it aside with a knife and dip your berries in one at a time. If the wax is too thick the berries will become much too big. When you find the wax is just the right thickness work as fast as you can to complete as much as possible. There is nothing more to do to the berries except paint small brown dots in the middle, and put a little green on the stems.

Cut leaves out from pattern No. 12, p. 90, in what proportion you wish. Tray wire together. Paint sap green and wax them.

Mount berries and leaves on tray wire stems to keep them thin and delicate as in Fig. 55.

Paint stems brown.

These snowberry stems can look amazingly life-like as the fruits in reality appear like tiny globes of wax. Their slight artificiality makes them both fanciful and out of the ordinary.

APRICOT BRANCH
Pattern 13, p. 90

Materials: cellulose wadding, 18-gauge floristry wire, reel wire (30-gauge), thin orange crêpe paper.

Three fruits and seven leaves per branch. Break up cellulose wadding into strips about ¾ in. wide (see p. 34). Take an 18-gauge wire (about 7 in. long) and start wrapping the wadding round the top. Bend over wire.

This is most important when making fruit as it will otherwise come straight off when you start waxing it.

Continue wrapping cellulose round wire as tightly and firmly as possible so that you build it up to a good round shape about the size as shown in pattern 13. To get the top surface as smooth as possible use the cellulose strips as thin as you are able.

The next stage is to put in the indentation. Take your reel wire and fix firmly on to stem as close to the fruit as possible. Wind over top of fruit and bring back to same place pulling it as tight as you can. Secure round stem and break off. Shape fruit with your hands some more if necessary. Cover very smoothly with $\frac{1}{2}$-in. orange crêpe paper binding.

Dip in hot wax two or three times until you have a smooth waxy finish

FIG. 56

with no paper showing. To give the effect of bloom, paint over wax with thin white paint and dab off with cellulose wadding or a paper hanky. Paint small brown dot at centre of fruit and brown on stem. Make leaves up in thin paper from pattern 13, p. 90. Bind down stems, paint green or brown and wax. Mount stem as shown in Fig. 56.

CHERRY BRANCHES
Pattern 14, p. 90

Materials: cellulose wadding, medium tray wire, pale yellow or deep bright red, thin crêpe paper.

Cut 6-in. lengths of tray wire for cherries. There are approximately eight cherries and seven leaves per branch.

Make fruit in same way as for apricots except for indentation. Build up to size shown in pattern 14. Bind in which colour you prefer as thin as you

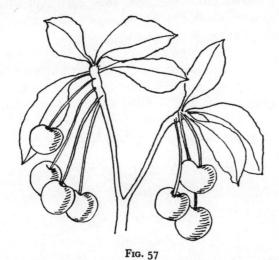

Fig. 57

possibly can. Wrap round and round wadding ball till you achieve a nice round shape. Stick bind unobtrusively at side of cherry. Bind down stem with very fine pale green crêpe paper binding. Dip once or twice in hot wax, for a smooth finish.

Paint over cream cherries with a little pinkish-red in one or two places and dab paint with a piece of wadding to get a natural blended appearance.

Paint over red cherries with a little crimson and magenta, if necessary, to enrich them Let paint get quite dry. As you will use paint rather thickly mix with terebine dryers to help speed up the drying process.

Brush over with shellac. Clean paint brush immediately with the methylated spirit.

Make up leaves in thin paper from pattern 14, p. 90. Bind down stems. Paint green, draw on some veins with white crayon. Mount fruit and leaves as shown in Fig. 57.

HIP SPRAYS
Pattern 15, p. 91

Materials: flame red thin crêpe paper, some thick duplex paper, cellulose wadding, medium tray wire.

Five hips and three leaves per spray.

Cut out sepals in thick crêpe paper. Cut 7-in. lengths of tray wire. Bind round top of wire (remembering to bend it over) a 2-in long strip of cellulose wadding. Stick in place with glue. Stick round this your sepal (see Fig. 58). Wrap more cellulose wadding round and over the base of calyx building up the shape of a hip as shown in pattern 15, p. 91. Cover with $\frac{1}{2}$-in. strip of red paper. Stick down without binding down stem.

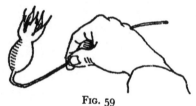

FIG. 58 FIG. 59

You now have to wax the hip and not the sepal on top so bend wire up (see Fig. 59). Dip into hot wax up to the sepal, two or three times to get a smooth coat. When wax is cool bend wire back again. Take wax off stem. Bend down stem in pale green crêpe paper.

Paint sepals dark brown. Brighten up colour of hip with a little cadmium red. Allow to dry out completely.

Brush over hip with shellac and wash brush in methylated spirit.

Make up leaves from pattern 15, p. 91, in thin crêpe paper (a dark green on top, a light green underneath). Serrate edges (see Chapter IX).

Wire with tray wire. Bind in sprays. Paint a little crimson lake on leaf tips and edges. Wax.

Mount leaves and fruit on to 18-gauge floristry wire (see Fig. 60). Paint stems brown, and shape them.

FIG. 60

When you are making fruit you need suitable containers to put them in, otherwise they easily spill over and get ruined.

Flower pots are perfectly suitable if you are making fruit on fairly substantial stems, but small things on tray wire need something that holds them more securely.

You can fill a plastic cup or pot with sand and wedge the wires into that. You can also put some florapak or similar material into a pot and the wires will stick in and hold quite well.

I hope the instructions in this chapter have given you some idea of the possibilities that wax and paper have for making fruit.

The fruit described is obviously only a simple beginning, and with a little ingenuity you can adapt these methods to making practically anything you wish. Moulding the basic shapes is obviously the hardest part and requires some practice, but with perseverance and good observation you may eventually try making larger fruits like pears and apples.

Try and bind the cellulose wadding really firmly with your fingertips so that the finished piece will not squash out of shape with the slightest pressure.

Always cover wadding shape with the smoothest possible layer of crêpe binding.

When you have finished the waxing, your scissors are an invaluable tool. Use them to scrape off any lumps of wax. The points will dig out wax round stem and the side edges can be used to make dents. If your finished waxing has not been quite so smooth as you would like, go over surface with a rag soaked in turpentine.

Don't be limited by what you have in the fruit bowl. Vegetables can be just as decorative as fruit. If you want to try making other things the choice is limitless.

If you have something real to look at nothing is impossible—from beans, peas, spring onions and carrots, to pomegranates, radishes and baby marrows.

CHAPTER XI

Stem Binding

Even if you have had a go at making many of the things in this book, you may not be quite certain how you actually put things together on longer stems.

When you are binding a short stem, say one foot long, there are no problems. Two or three 18-gauge floristry wires will be quite sufficient to hold in a rigid position anything you wish. It is when you require a long stem between 2 and 3 ft. that the difficulties arise. You will need a stronger, heavier piece of wire, especially if the flowers and leaves are waxed and therefore much heavier.

For this purpose use a thick piece of galvanized wire and mount it into your stem a little way from the top. If you want a very tall and straight flower stem, you can use a wooden dahlia stick or split bamboo cane.

If you want to make long trailing stems, you can use centre-cane (as used in basket-making). This makes very light flexible stems and has the advantage of being cheap to buy.

When you are binding with a strip of crêpe paper, cut in a strip about 1 in. wide and use doubled over for extra strength.

Floratape or guttapercha makes a much smoother finish but you can only buy a few colours, none of which look very realistic. Unfortunately you cannot paint over it very easily, but it is of course quite waterproof and you will be able to stand the stems in water if you wish.

Crêpe paper binding can be painted over in any colour and can be matched exactly with shaded and blended colours. The only disadvantage is that the ridges of the binding will always show, however tightly and skilfully you wind it round.

If you are mounting something small into a stem, say a leaf or a bud, you need simply wrap binding round the two stems and continue on down (see Fig. 61). If you are putting in something heavier, like a flower or another stem, you must wrap your binding several times round the two stems, then squeeze really tight with thumb and first finger before you continue binding down stem. This will give added strength to what is often a weak spot. It is very irritating to curve a flower or stem out from main branch, and then find the binding breaking up.

FIG. 61

If you are mounting stems with paper always remember to stick it down at the bottom. Floratape and guttapercha is self-sealing.

It is well worth adding small details to stem work whenever possible to make them more interesting. If there are ridges put them in; if there are aerial roots cut up some string and mount it in. Geranium stems have little tiny leaflets growing at the base of the leaves, and other stems have spots and even stripes. If you are making roses you can even make paper thorns and stick them on. Why not? It all helps.

CHAPTER XII

Flowers to Make for Parties

Ⅰt is possible, with literally a few handfuls of bright paper, to make a marvellous dazzle of flower-like colour. Remembering that most people will be looking more at each other than your decorations anyway, you can get away with the minimum of effort for the maximum effect. If the lighting is going to be dim make sure they show by having them in the brightest colours you can get.

The method you use to make them should be as simple as possible, so that you can quickly rustle up vast quantities in next to no time. The largest size you can make them in will obviously produce the most impact.

If you want flowers on single stems (you can mount them on flower canes) make them up to 12 in. in diameter.

If you are going to join them up in garlands, 6 in. in diameter would be a good average size.

CRÊPE PAPER HIBISCUS-TYPE FLOWERS

Without removing paper from cover, cut crossways into four, three or two strips depending on what size flower you want to make. The small strips would be best for garlands. The large ones will be very large flowers. Remove cover. Cut down one side with your scissors as shown in Fig. 62. Using about half of the length, screw and pleat the straight edge round and round to form the flower. Bind round end with thick reel wire and leave enough wire to join with other flowers if making garlands. Shape flower by stretching out paper to look like petals and frill all the edges. Flowers can be made to look more subtle if you wash them over with a brush that has

73

been wetted with water. This makes the colour run. It will look good when the paper has dried out, but you may need to give the flowers another shaping.

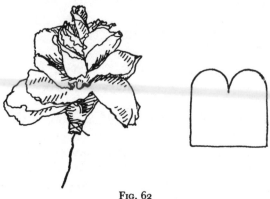

FIG. 62

TISSUE PAPER ROSE-TYPE FLOWERS

Lay out twenty to twenty-four layers of tissue paper. All one colour, except about eight on top which should be a shade lighter or darker.

Draw round pattern, exactly the same shape as Fig. 63, but in any size you

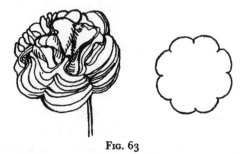

FIG. 63

like. Pin middle and cut out. Remove pin and screw round centre of paper to form a vertical shape. Pleat the paper to look like petals, especially at the centre. Poke hole in centre of paper, and put a wire through it, which has been bent over at the top. With thick reel wire, wire round base of flower on

74

to central wire. To make sure it is secure, thread it through some of the paper first. To shape flower, separate the layers of paper to give a giant puff-ball effect. Pleat the paper again to give the appearance of petals.

CHAPTER XIII

Christmas Bits and Pieces, and How to Fix Them

Decemeber stirs most people into action, and enthusiasm for making the Christmas decorations. Each year one has every good intention of doing something entirely different, and yet one so often ends up with last year's bits and pieces because it seems wasteful not to use them again and yet again.

If you are tired of doing this there are lots of things that can be done to change and rejuvenate existing acquisitions. Then, by adding something that is quite new, you can re-create decorations that are completely fresh and up-to-date.

On the other hand, you may find that you enjoy making your own decorations for Christmas so that you prefer to renew them every year. So much the better: this is obviously an ideal to strive for because really half the point of decorating a table, Christmas tree, mantelpiece or room is that you should transform them. You will not manage this very well, unless you radically change your approach every time you start out to do it.

There are so many ways to add Christmas sparkle to quite ordinary materials that you can buy cheaply at Christmastime. Plastic ferns, and fruit, dried twigs and leaves, empire-made birds and bells, can all be treated with a little varnish, paint or glitter and be converted into something gay, rich-looking and original.

Firstly choose a scheme of colour and stick to it throughout.

Scarlet, cerise and gold.

Peacock blues-greens and silver.

Lime, copper and bronze.

Silver and gold.

Try making your own decorations for the Christmas tree and repeat them on the Christmas table too. Hunt around the shops while there is still a wide selection available and try not to leave the operation too close to Christmas Day, or you will find yourself glittering the turkey.

One of your aims should be simplicity. Don't have too much clutter going on, but what you do make, have as rich and Christmassy as possible.

You can make any of the flowers described in the preceding chapters but make them up in fabulous colours and materials. Mount stems in silver cellotape or cellophane.

At Christmas there is complete justification for faking nature from all points of view. Forget about realism and concentrate on making things shimmer and glisten. I list below some materials that will help you to do this. A list of stockists is at the end of the book.

Gold and silver paint in aerosols.

Glitter and adhesive gum to stick it on with.

Sequins, jewels, beads and buttons.

Tinsel.

Transparent glass painting colour and methylated spirit.

Cellophane, metallic crêpe paper and other attractive Christmas paper.

Fabrics (fine, stiffened).

Ribbons.

Cellotape (transparent and silver).

Christmas tree glass balls.

Picture hanging wire for stems.

You can buy a large range of sizes and colours in 'Glitters'. Perhaps I had better explain that this is the name for the tiny bits of sparkle that land on practically all manufactured Christmas decorations. You will find gold and silver the most useful colours by far, and for most work a combination of the two is the most successful and pretty way of using it: you can stick it on with varnish but the most efficient method is with adhesive gum.

Sequins can be stuck on in just the same way as the glitter. You will not need to use many. Using one colour only, stick them on here and there to give extra richness to the glitter.

A simple way to enable you to use ribbon or fabrics for making petals and leaves is to stick your covered wire down the centre with cellotape. You can buy all sorts of beautiful types of ribbon and for Christmas decorations

77

particularly, you can make sprays of leaves and flowers that look quite different from anything that you can buy in a shop. You may also find wired ribbon useful if you simply want to tie it into bows, because the wire will enable you to give it a fixed shape.

Clusters of Christmas roses, tied with a few leaves, candles and a bit of ribbon can look very pretty decorating the Christmas tree.

Jewels, beads, large sequins and buttons are mentioned for their possibilities as glamorous stamens for flower centres. Large imitation stones make good lily stamen anthers and clusters of tiny silver or pearl beads can be put on to wire and made into rose centres, berries and so on.

Transparent glass painting colour will help you paint over anything that would be improved by the addition of a shiny coloured finish.

Many cheap plastic sprays of fern, holly, mistletoe and beech leaves have excellent shape and line, but are rather dull and unexciting in colour and texture. If you paint them over with these extremely vivid colours of Prussian blue, green and amber, then add glitter, you will enrich them beyond recognition.

In the following pages I describe in more detail some ideas for you to try. I suggest you do a few to get the hang of the techniques and then, probably, you will be anxious to adapt them to your own inventions.

WHITE MUSLIN LILY

Buy any fine white material that has a certain amount of stiffness to it. You will only need one layer of cloth for your flower petals. Cut them out from pattern 16, p. 91.

Three large petals
Three small petals

Cover six 20-gauge × 10-in. floristry wires with $\frac{1}{4}$-in. white crêpe paper binding. Stick these down the centre of petals with cellotape, and trim surplus off if necessary. Paste all round edge on top side of petals about $\frac{1}{4}$ in. Dust liberally with gold glitter, and allow to dry.

Make six gold stamens as described in Chapter V (see Figs. 28 and 29) about 5-in. length to stick out of flower. Anthers can be made out of jewels or large gold sequins. Cover thick floristry wire in gold for the pistil, allowing

6 in. to stick out from flower. Wire stamens and pistil on to a length of thick galvanized wire.

Next wire round the three large petals as evenly as possible. Then wire round the small ones to fit between them.

Bind down stem in gold.

Curve the petals back. Bend the stamens over slightly.

TREE WITH BIRDS' NESTS

Cut down a branch of wood with numerous tiny twigs and the overall shape of a miniature tree. Spray all over with silver paint. When dry glue on glitter, especially on tips of offshoots.

Make five small birds' nests with moss and reel wire.

Attach to branches of tree. Fill them with tiny silver Christmas tree balls, which make the birds' eggs.

This tree would look equally pretty in gold.

METALLIC CRÊPE PAPER ROSES

Use extra thick crêpe metallic paper in silver, gold, green, red or pink, and bought stamens if possible.

From pattern 17, p. 91, cut

   Two small petals
   Three medium petals
   Five large petals

Wire a bunch of stamens on to a thick floristry wire and paint to match the paper. When dry wire round the petals. First the two small ones opposite each other, then the medium ones as evenly spaced round as possible and finally the large ones, each one overlapping the preceding one. Bind down stem in same paper as flower.

To shape flower, spread out stamens in centre. Stretch each petal across between first finger and thumb of each hand, especially at the base. Roll edge of petal either with the fingers or over a knitting needle. Stretch rolled edges with finger and thumb to achieve a loose, natural look. Curve stem.

CHRISTMAS WEEPING WILLOW TREE

Buy five to seven sprays of plastic fern. The less fussy it is the better. Mount together to make a small tree about 2 ft. high, as Fig. 64. Keep the main stem slender and curve it to give it a slight twist. Next paint on your coloured

FIG. 64

glass paint, and allow to dry. Then stick on plenty of glitter and on the tips of the branches a few matching sequins. If you like you can buy a cheap Christmas robin, give it the same sort of treatment and fix it on to one of the branches.

80

Fix tree into flower pot or container with a wedge of plasticine.

This tree would look good in shades of blue and green, brown and gold, or white and silver.

CHRISTMAS VINE

You will need silver beads (size 6 and 8 if possible), thin white crêpe paper and silver cellotape.

Per spray from pattern No. 18, p. 92

Five leaves

Eighteen beads (approx.)—four size 6 and fourteen size 8

Three tendrils

Cut out leaves (allowing two layers per leaf) and serrate the edges. Stick 20-gauge floristry wire or white tray wire down centre allowing 6 in. for stem. Also stick a support wire at bottom of leaf.

Bind down stems with $\frac{1}{4}$-in. wide silver cellotape.

FIG. 65

Put each bead on to a short length of reel wire. When it is halfway down wire take two ends together between thumb and forefinger and twist bead around and around until it is firmly held by the wire. Twist them into bunches of three with three small ones together.

Then mount them up to the shape of a bunch of grapes with the small ones at the top.

For your tendrils cut three 7-in. lengths of white tray wire. Cover with ¼-in. wide silver cellotape. Twist round and round fine knitting needle for corkscrew effect.

Paint lots of fine veins on your leaves in brown.

Mount as Fig. 65 with silver cellotape on a length of tray wire or thin galvanized wire.

N.B. If you can buy red beads this spray might look very rich made with crimson leaves and red cellotape.

If you want to make realistic flowers especially for Christmas the one I strongly advocate is the Christmas rose. They are not easy flowers to come by, and if you are fortunate enough to see them in the florists in December, they are usually rather expensive. One therefore feels in no way cheating if one mixes a few handmade flowers with real holly and mistletoe, ivy or other evergreen for a simple but essentially Christmassy arrangement. The directions for making them are as follows:

CHRISTMAS ROSE

Cut five petals and two sepals from pattern 19, p. 92, in thick white crêpe paper.

Cover a thick floristry wire and bend top over ¼ in. Take a bunch of string and wire round as tightly as possible. Wire round petals as evenly as you can, and so that they overlap. Stick sepals opposite at base of flower. Thicken stem with a little cellulose wadding and cover with white crêpe paper binding.

Trim string middle flat on top so that it sticks out about 3 in. Spread out string and paint pale green. When dry paint top of string with thick lemon yellow. Paint stem and sepals pale green. Run pale crimson round edges of sepal and down stem, over the green. When paint is dry shape petals, by stretching between thumbs and fingers.

Bend flower heads over.

These flowers are much improved by a coat of wax.

Another flower which many people like at Christmas because of its vivid scarlet flowers is poinsettia, and although to my mind it does not quite add up to a Dickensian Christmas, it certainly combines effectively with holly, candles, etc.

POINSETTIA

Although it is important to shape these flowers accurately, I don't think there is much point in making them look realistic. They will make livelier decoration if you use a vivid rich material such as flocked paper or cellophane. What look like red petals are in fact red leaves which turn to green down the stem. It is therefore a good idea to buy your material in green as well as red. The flowers are in a tiny cluster at the top. A pretty way to make these is with gold beads but you may find something else that looks equally well.

From pattern 20, p. 92, cut out:

Three small red leaves

Four medium red leaves

Three large red leaves

Three green leaves

Have eight beads per stem.

Put each bead on to a short length of reel wire. When it is halfway down wire take the two ends together between thumb and forefinger and twist bead around and around until it is firmly held by the wire.

Mount the beads into three clusters.

Cover thick floristry wires with red and green paper. Stick down the backs of your red and green leaves.

Mount your flowers (beads) and leaves on to a length of thick galvanized wire with dark green paper. The beads should be placed very close together at the top. The red leaves circled round them and the green leaves are put in down the stem.

You may like a few tips on arranging artificial flowers. First, don't worry about any rules you may have learnt for arranging the real ones. Try to forget them. The most important thing is to have a completely fresh approach.

There is nothing to prevent you making one or two ENORMOUS flowers

Fig. 66

and standing them on their own in the corner of the room. You can also fill a basket or similar container full to overflowing with paper roses and leave the flower heads just sticking out on top.

If you decide to make a more formal arrangement with a variety of flowers, leaves and fruit, you will probably find them a little easier than real ones to arrange.

This is because they have wires throughout, which can be bent at will to go in any direction and stay put. Do not, however, neglect this latter task. A lot depends on the overall final shaping of the stems in an arrangement of artificial sprays as to whether you achieve the natural flow and slightly haphazard look of real flowers and foliage (see Fig. 66).

To fix your sprays into their container you can use the conventional chicken-wire method, but you will find the addition of some dried moss helpful. Wired stems can get rather heavy and need more support than real flowers. Cut a piece of chicken-wire and snip off outside thickened wire. Put a wadge of moss to cover it, loosen it with the fingers. Then turn chicken-wire over it all round edge. Roll up into loose ball. Pack into container so that it fits fairly tightly. You will find it possible to fix quite heavy stems firmly by this method.

You can very simply make 'swags' of fruit, vegetables or flowers. These loosely put-together strings are a useful form of decoration, either to hang on a wall or put on a table.

You make up the fruit or vegetables like a string of French onions. Get plenty of natural coloured raffia and knot it at the top. Start plaiting it and take in the stems of fruit or vegetables every few inches, when you have made it as long as you require knot the raffia to finish off the bottom. If you are putting flowers together for a table decoration you must wire them together as invisibly as possible with reel wire.

Japanese arranging methods can be very effective, using a few artificial sprays on a flat dish or plate. It is necessary to stick them down with a plastic cement. This is a very strong type of glue which means that the arrangement is rather permanent. You will need about an inch of the stems to lie flat on the dish (see Fig. 67). Put plenty of glue on the dish and the stems and keep in place with heavy weights while it is drying. When glue is set quite hard you can cover up the base by sticking on some bits of moss and a few pebbles.

To put a plant in a flower pot so that it is quite firm and stable, first line the bottom of the pot with a little newspaper. Measure the plant in the pot to see that the stem is the right height, and bend the wire up an inch at the bottom to secure it.

Mix some sand and cement (which you can buy ready mixed in small bags) with a little water. Put plant in centre of pot. Put mixture all round it up to an inch at the top.

When dried out, cover with moss or peat.

FIG. 67

Finally, don't be afraid to copy ideas. The best way to learn is from other people's efforts. Look around whenever you can to see what other people are making, and find out how they have made it.

Your own ideas will develop and grow from this stimulus faster than you would think possible.

As in any book on how to do something, I have written this as a series of natural progressions, starting with simple processes and building up to more complicated ones.

It is very desirable, perhaps important even, to roughly read it through from beginning to end. It is only when you have a good idea of the whole that you can use the book just as a list of instructions, each one complete in itself—which is why I put this in right at the end of the book!

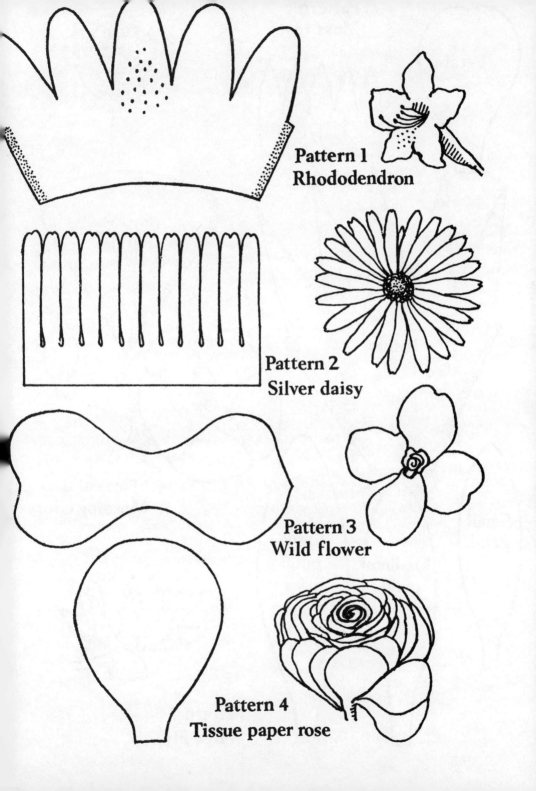

Pattern 1
Rhododendron

Pattern 2
Silver daisy

Pattern 3
Wild flower

Pattern 4
Tissue paper rose

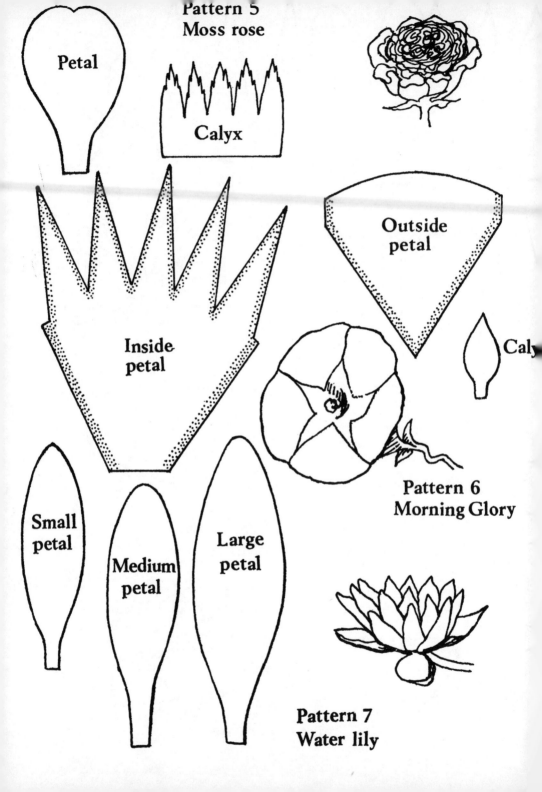

Pattern 5
Moss rose

Petal

Calyx

Outside petal

Inside petal

Cal

Small petal

Medium petal

Large petal

Pattern 6
Morning Glory

Pattern 7
Water lily

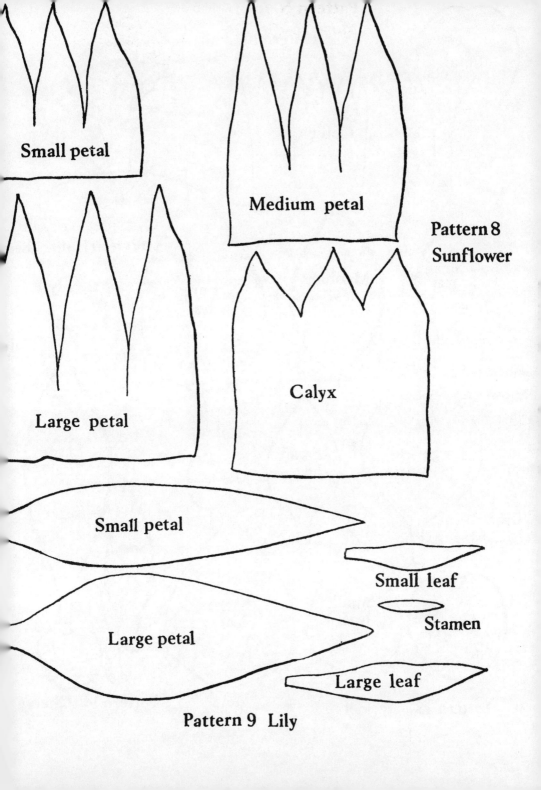

Small petal

Medium petal

Pattern 8
Sunflower

Large petal

Calyx

Small petal

Small leaf

Large petal

Stamen

Large leaf

Pattern 9 Lily

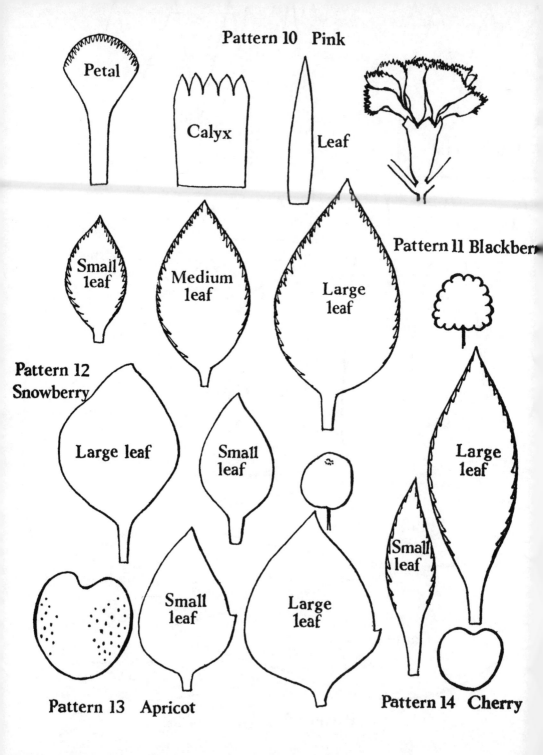

Pattern 10 Pink

Petal

Calyx

Leaf

Small leaf

Medium leaf

Large leaf

Pattern 11 Blackberry

Pattern 12 Snowberry

Large leaf

Small leaf

Large leaf

Small leaf

Small leaf

Large leaf

Pattern 13 Apricot

Pattern 14 Cherry

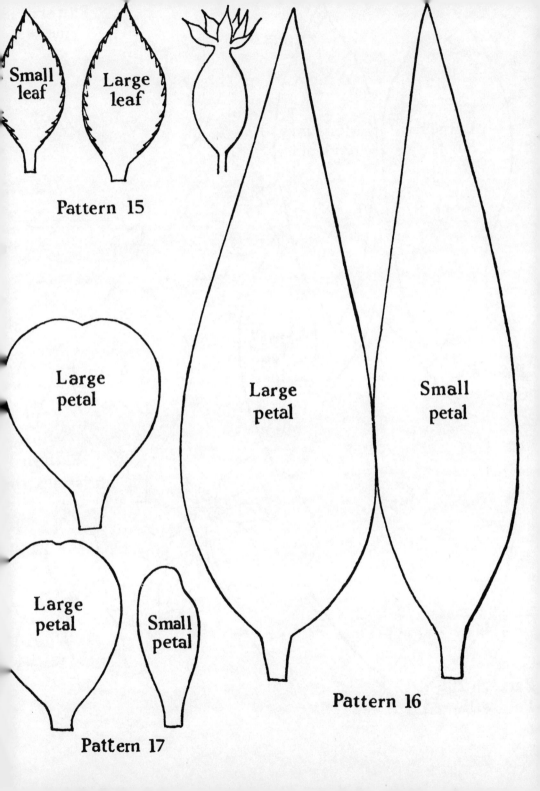

Small
leaf

Large
leaf

Pattern 15

Large
petal

Large
petal

Small
petal

Large
petal

Small
petal

Pattern 16

Pattern 17

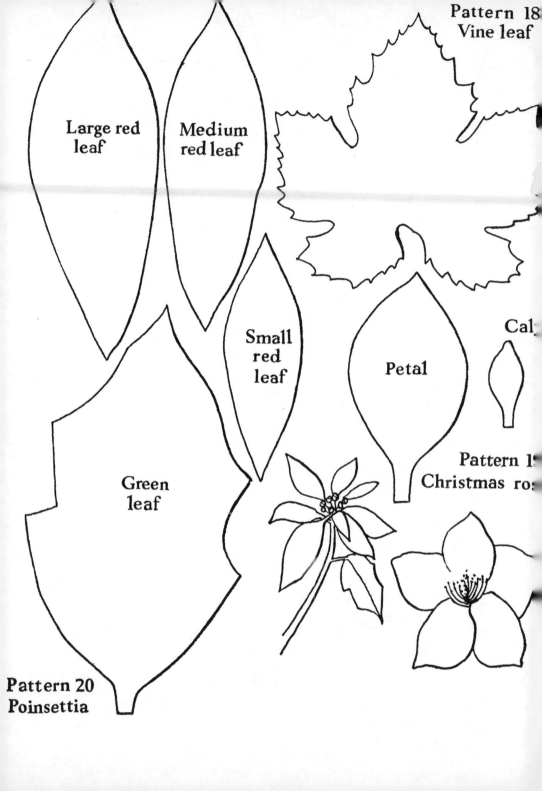

Pattern 18
Vine leaf

Large red leaf

Medium red leaf

Small red leaf

Petal

Cal

Green leaf

Pattern 1
Christmas ro

Pattern 20
Poinsettia

Source Index

Beads and sequins	The Beadshop, 53 South Molton Street, London, W. 1
	Department stores
Cane	Dryad Ltd., 22 Bloomsbury Street, London, W.C.1
Cellulose wadding	Chemist
Cement and sand	Hardware shop
Chicken-wire	Hardware shop
Cork bark	Florist
Dried material	Selfridges Ltd., Oxford Street, London, W.1
Floratape (or Guttapercha)	Florist
Florapak	Florist
Glitter	Handicraft shop
Glue or Adhesive gum	Do-it-yourself shop or Hardware shop
Casco Glue-all	Do-it-yourself shop or Hardware shop
Gloy Multiglue, Copydex	Hardware shop or stationers
Moss	Florist
Paints and brushes (Student's sable Nos. 2–7 ox hair Nos. 9–12)	Art shop
Glass Painting colour	Art shop
Silver and Gold Aerosol Spray	Woolworths
Papers of all descriptions	F. G. Kettle, 127 High Holborn, London, W.C.1
	Paperchase, 216 Tottenham Court Road, London WC1
Dennison's crêpe and cellophane	Stationers and art shop
Plastic flowers and fruit	Department stores, Woolworths
Raffia	Handicraft shop
Scissors:	
Florist's scissors	Hardware shop
Pointed surgical scissors	Chemist
Shellac	Hardware shop or Woolworths
Sea fern, coral and shells	Sarogny Art Products, 11 Craneford Way, Twickenham, Middx.

Sea fern, coral and shells	The Eaton Bag Co. Ltd., 16 Manette Street, London, W.1
	Aquariums
Stamens (by post)	Priscilla Lobley Flower Kits, Thorpe Lodge, Ealing Green, London, W.5
String (coarse sizal as for packing parcels)	Woolworths or Hardware shop
Turpentine substitute	Woolworths or Hardware shop
Wax, candles (clear white)	Hardware shop
Paraffin wax	Campbell Technical Waxes, Thames Road, Crayford, Kent

Wire:

Floristry stub wire (22-gauge fine) (20-gauge medium) (18-gauge thick)	Florist
Reel wire (36-gauge fine) (30-gauge medium) (24-gauge thick)	Florist
Floral wire	Hardware shop
Cotton covered tray wire (24-gauge medium)	Priscilla Lobley Flower Kits, Thorpe Lodge, Ealing Green, London, W.5
Galvanized wire (20-gauge fine) (16-gauge medium) (12-gauge thick)	Hardware shop
Picture hanging stranded brass wire	Hardware shop
Millinery covered wire white	John Lewis & Co. Ltd., Oxford Street, London, W.1
Thick crêpe paper, stamens wire etc. Flower-making sundries (by post)	Priscilla Lobley Flower Kits, Thorpe Lodge, Ealing Green, London, W.5

Christmas Suppliers

Barnum's (Carnival novelties) Ltd. 67 Hammersmith Road, London, W.14	Glitters, papers, sequins, beads, etc.
Constance Spry Ltd., 98 Marylebone Lane, W.1	Paper, plastic leaves, ribbons and glitter, and florist's sundries.

Method Index

(In order of working)